Still Learning to Love

Still Learning to Love

MARTIN HALLETT

Published by
HOW Publications
c/o PO Box 13, Prenton, Wirral CH43 6YB

First published in 1987 as *I Am Learning to Love* by Marshall Morgan and Scott Publications Ltd.

This revised edition © 2004 Martin Hallett

All rights reserved. No part of this publication may be reproduced or transmitted in any form or by any means, electronic or mechanical, including photocopying, recording or any information storage or retrieval system, without prior permission in writing from the publishers.

ISBN 0-9539283-1-4

Designed and typeset by Kenneth Burnley, Wirral, Cheshire.
Printed in Great Britain by TJ International Ltd, Padstow, Cornwall.

Contents

	Foreword	vii
	Introduction	ix
1	Schooldays	1
2	A New Lifestyle	11
3	A New Friend	21
4	A Child in Christ	32
5	Love Often Hurts	43
6	Vision of a Ministry	51
7	Growth of a Ministry	61
8	Crisis of Faith – What Does the Bible Say?	75
9	Growing in the Ministry	84
10	Vision of a Family	96
11	The Family – Hurting and Healing	103
12	Taking a Journey	110
13	Tragedy Strikes	115
14	Life Changes	122
15	Time For a Move	130
16	Hope and Healing?	135

Foreword

MARTIN HALLETT is a most extraordinary person. Not a professional academic but, which is far rarer nowadays, a profound thinker. Not a husband and father but, most unusually in the modern world, a genuine friend.

He is a Christian. He is also a homosexual. He is unashamedly, positively, proudly grateful for his faith; and he is unashamedly, positively, proudly grateful for his homosexual identity too. He sees his sexuality, as he sees his salvation, as a gift from God. And there is no contradiction between the two.

This open, honest and moving account tells how Martin discovered his sexual orientation as a teenager, of his conversion to Christ as a young man, and of his subsequent life and work. It also tells of his search for love and intimacy, and how that search was fulfilled. And how his love of Christ resulted in his celibate lifestyle without any denial of his orientation. He speaks with the confidence of one who is totally accepted, profoundly loved, and utterly fulfilled.

As I write, the Church is, according to the newspapers, being torn apart by the issue of sexuality. We are all supposed to be in one camp – as it were – or the other: for inclusiveness or for morality; pro-gay or pro-marriage; for our time or for the Bible. Compassionate or principled. Martin (like Jesus Himself) is both. He knows what it is to be gay, and he cares passionately about scripture. I cannot help thinking that if we were all to listen to him for long enough we would get on much better together. (But then, of course, that would be true if we were to listen to His Master too . . .)

Martin has often corrected me, surprised me, or simply stopped me in my tracks. He has also astonished me with his instinctive theological insights. I never listen to him without learning something

Foreword

new . . . which is more than I could say of most of the preachers and teachers of the Church.

I don't just recommend his book. I recommend Martin himself. Meet him in these pages and you will be challenged and changed for life.

ANNE ATKINS

Introduction

IN 1985 I WROTE *I Am Learning To Love*, which was a fairly honest account of my life up that point. Sadly we never made the film with Tom Cruise! Needless to say, a lot has happened in my life since then and this is an attempt to share it as my story. There are five completely new chapters, and those from the original book have been revamped and expanded. The way I now express myself is very different. When I read the early version it reminded me at times of an Adrian Plass caricature, much to my embarrassment. I'm not sure if it's a cultural, social or spiritual change in me. Many Christians said how much the original book encouraged and helped them, which was always a great blessing to me. If this one has the same response I'll be thrilled – if not, I know a good therapist!

In True Freedom Trust (T*f*T) we encourage people to value their story. If we believe our story is valuable, we should believe that we are valuable too. This is my story to date, and I hope something of what I've learned through it about God, myself and other people. It's about love, or at least about my attempt to receive it and express it. In my own experience of learning to love, many significant people have influenced, encouraged, empowered and suffered with me. Some of them are mentioned in this book. I am grateful to them all of course, including my mother, father and brother, Roy, Ian, John, Gill, Chris, David, Mike, Annette, Jane, Martin B, Douglas, Nigel, Linda, and Peter, who deserves a special mention because he let me share some of his own story, which has influenced mine and my ministry so much.

The last few years have seen a lot of growth in T*f*T, and people like Martin D, Chris and Dan have been a wonderful encouragement and support to me, but also largely responsible for the growth and development of our ministry. The trustees of T*f*T have always been brilliant in coping with some difficult situations. In the early

Introduction

days there were Roy, Ian, Dave, Malcolm and Charles. Now we have John and Tricia, Peter and Jean, and more recently Sheila, Stefan, Jeremy, Kim and Jonathan – the last four bringing a young influence to T*f*T's future. Finally, Walter as our chairman has been a source of support and encouragement, along with his wife Sylvia, for many years as a friend and trustee.

I am very grateful for all the help and hard work that Martin D, Chris and Dan have given on this book, reading the script and correcting it so many times.

I have known Ken and Gill Burnley since I first became involved in St Mary's, Upton. Ken is responsible for editing and publishing this book and has lovingly given his skill and time to make this project happen, for which all of us in T*f*T are grateful.

Finally, when I asked the well-known Christian writer and broadcaster, Anne Atkins, if she would like to write the Foreword, she agreed, even though her busy schedule made it quite difficult. When I saw what Anne had written, I was stunned. 'Does she know what I'm really like?' Thank you Anne for your amazing comments and your support of our ministry.

I pray that God will speak to you through my story. It will not be in the same way as he has spoken to me, but if you feel more valued and loved by God as a result, my prayer is answered positively.

1
Schooldays

I T WAS MY FIRST TASTE OF BOARDING SCHOOL. I had been a 'day boy' since the age of seven, but now, at thirteen I was boarding for the first time. Large Victorian buildings, many of them converted houses, formed a major part of the school's property, but they had been supplemented by one or two more modern buildings. The campus extended over fifteen acres, situated in an older part of Liverpool suburbia. I had lived in this area all my life. It was very familiar territory, except for the boarding houses in the school, which seemed another world.

The dormitory was large, old and drab, with 30 iron-framed beds in two rows, facing each other. Each bed, with its own bedside cupboard, was devoid of anything at all homely. Regular inspections by the prefects made sure that the white cotton sheets and coarse blankets were made up meticulously by the envelope method, without unnecessary folds or creases. As we all prepared for bedtime I was filled with a sense of fear, dreading what further horrors the night could bring. It seemed like a nightmare from which I could never awake.

Eventually, having bathed and changed into pyjamas, it was time to get into bed. It had been my turn to use one of the four Victorian baths. Thankfully, I remembered to test the amount of water by sticking my thumb on top of the plug. The water was to be no higher than my wrist. We were also carefully timed, so that we would not try to relax and luxuriate in the two inches or so of hot water. We were made to shower after all sport activities, which took place nearly every day, so we were not really all that dirty.

The lights went out and for a moment or two there was silence. My fear was beginning to increase and I could feel my heart thumping under the bedclothes.

Then a voice from the dark corner of the dorm said, 'Let's have a "cage". Who shall we do tonight?'

Still Learning to Love

My heart missed a beat. 'Oh please God, let it not be me!'
'What about Hallett?' another voice said menacingly.
'Stand up on your bed, Hallett.'
As I nervously stood on the bed a torchlight shone through the darkness. It was followed by one or two others and then they focused their beams on my eyes. In a strange way the dazzling glare from the torchlights provided a physical distraction which somehow relieved just a little of the tension.
'What shall we make him do?'
'I know! . . . Drop your trousers!'
I obeyed immediately, trying not to appear as terrified as I knew I was.
'Now, what will they ask me to do?' I wondered.
'You really are the lowest of the low, aren't you?' the menacing voice continued.
'Say yes, you horrible creature!' someone else chipped in.
I did not reply. I hoped I would play this right and not encourage them to continue. Perhaps if they didn't think I was frightened they would stop.
'You have been seen talking to the day boys again. You know that's not permitted.'
I remained silent.
There seemed to be a little uneasiness. Someone was coming. 'Get back in your bed!' shouted one of the boys.
The torches went out and I obeyed. Seconds later the prefect came in and got into bed. At last I felt a bit more secure. He was the head prefect of the school and seemed more gentle, fair and sensitive than the others. I had to clean his shoes for him once as a minor punishment, and was struck by his lack of arrogance, compared to most of the others. I knew he was one of the few people in the boarding house whom I could look up to and admire. He had all the necessary qualities; he was mature, a good sportsman, tall and quite good looking.
As I lay in bed, I began to wonder how on earth I could ever escape from this seemingly endless nightmare. Up to this point, my life as a day boy had been very enjoyable. I had a few close friends who lived within cycling distance of our house. We lived only a couple of miles from the school itself, which made commuting by bike very easy. In fact, latterly, I was travelling home for lunch, which made a nice break in the day. We often had three-mile runs,

after lessons at 4.30, but on three afternoons a week we had to play rugger or cricket, which would mean arriving home earlier. Saturdays were taken up with classes in the morning and sport in the afternoon. Membership of one of the cadet brigades was compulsory and most of us were in the Combined Cadet Force, which was run as close to military standards as possible. As a day boy, I quite enjoyed the CCF as it was called – we were able to have quite a bit of fun and sometimes 'send up' our superior officers. It was a combination of the old television series, *The Army Game* and *Dad's Army*. The punishments both in the CCF and at school were generally quite severe, but we were able to take them in our stride. I was not a particularly naughty boy but I enjoyed playing pranks with my mates. There was always a very strong sense of 'fair play' and 'being a good sport'. Telling tales was out of the question and one was always loyal to one's friends.

The reason for a sudden change in my situation was because mother and father had bought a share in a farm, with my uncle, aunt and cousin. It was about 35 miles from Liverpool, in Cheshire. The farmhouse was a magnificent mansion, with enough rooms for both families to be self-contained and still have space to spare. It was an exciting contrast to the three-bedroomed detached suburban house with which I was familiar.

What made the transition to life as a boarder more difficult was the fact that my parents did not actually move to Cheshire until I had been boarding for a few weeks. This meant I would go home whenever possible in my free time, even though it was out of bounds. We were only allowed to travel within a radius of one mile around the school buildings, and I felt really disorientated visiting my familiar home territory and then having to return to school after only an hour or so. Also, when I was a day boy, it never registered with me that the boarders had made up their own rule of refusing to associate with day boys, a rule I was eventually to transgress.

My brother was an old boy of the school, but because he was thirteen years older than me, he had left long before I had started. He was an actor and occasionally appeared on television and radio. This boosted my ego no end and it obviously impressed the other boys and masters as well. When I became a boarder, his success didn't help me at all, perhaps because he had been a day boy.

I often felt drawn to other boys and the younger masters at

school, especially anyone good at sport. One of my best friends, Tony, was an active sportsman and often encouraged me to play more effectively. I never really enjoyed sport or was successful at it; I mostly joined in to be accepted. Many times I would see Tony and his friends with their arms around each other. I longed for him to relate to me like that – but he did not.

Even the teacher I admired seemed to be playfully affectionate with other boys, but not with me. Someone announced that people who liked men more than women were homosexuals. I found myself blushing because it seemed to describe the way I felt. In fact I could remember having a 'crush' on Richard Burton and Laurence Harvey, whom I met through my brother when I was only seven. Now, at thirteen I found a book at home on sexuality and read that boys go through a homosexual stage. It crossed my mind that I might grow out of these feelings, although I was not totally convinced this would happen. Sexual activity with other boys was out of the question for me. I am not sure I even wanted it very much, it seemed 'dirty'.

Academically, I was lazy and usually accused of not realising my full potential. Unlike my brother, who excelled academically, I was never very far from the bottom of the 'C' stream class. I was often compared to him unfavourably, although I now realise how much I admired him. His strong charismatic personality was something I wanted, but did not have. I think he, in turn, may have felt threatened by my arrival, after thirteen years as a fairly demanding only child. I was very much a dreamer, with my head often in the clouds, imagining I had the charisma and eloquence of my extrovert brother.

So I lay in my hard dormitory bed, wondering how my relatively happy childhood could have turned to dark despair. My parents knew how I felt, as did the house-master. They were all very sympathetic and felt something should be done to change the situation. The widowed mother of a friend of mine offered to let me stay with them during term time so that I could become a day boy again. This seemed to be the answer to my prayers, but the headmaster refused to allow it. Despite encouragement from my father and mother to 'try and stick it out, there's a good lad', I was desperately unhappy. The only strength I seemed to have in this situation was mastering the art of avoiding tears and other physical expressions of my emotions. After years of practice I was very good at not crying.

Schooldays

What a terrible mistake many in this generation made in over-emphasising a 'stiff upper lip' attitude to every emotional trauma: we suffer for it later.

I may have been quiet, shy and timid but I felt determined that somehow I must do something to bring this nightmare to an end. I decided to run away. Having made the decision to go, it was a few days before I plucked up enough courage to do anything about it. Mother and father had moved to Cheshire by this time and I had nowhere I felt I could escape to. Then one Saturday afternoon was declared free of games. I found myself walking to the station, empty-handed and with hardly any money in my pocket. I very nervously enquired about a train to Chester and was told that if I left my name and address with the station authorities they would send the bill for the train fare to my parents. I felt a sense of tense excitement and relief, as well as some anxiety, as I made the hour-long train journey to Chester. It was about twelve miles from there to my new home, on a very busy main road. I walked a few miles to the first village and then stopped there, gazing into the river from a pretty road bridge. The full implications of what I was doing started to dawn on me. I wanted to cry, but could not. The best I could manage was a moan and gasp of breath! I continued to walk, then a motorist stopped and offered me a lift, taking me to the end of the long sweeping drive to the house. By this time it was dark and in the shadow of the many shrubberies surrounding the very large front lawn, I was able to sneak unnoticed around the side of the house and then through an open back door. I crept up to the top floor and hid in the attic. There I stayed for what seemed like an eternity. I felt secure, it no longer seemed like quite such a bad dream. Eventually I decided to creep into my bedroom, again hopefully unnoticed. Once in bed, I tried to sleep. Mother and father came into the bedroom and said very little, apart from, 'Well, you're a fine one! We'll have to sort this out in the morning. It's too late now . . . We've been very worried!' This must have been an understatement – the school had phoned earlier to ask if they knew my whereabouts!

My parents were sympathetic but took me back to school on the Monday and straight to the headmaster, who said he was prepared to take me back and would not punish me severely, provided I promised not to run away again. As that was a promise I said could not be kept and he still refused to let me become a day boy, it was agreed that I should leave the school. I felt a tremendous sense of relief.

We went to see the Cheshire education authorities and found that I would only be eligible for the local secondary modern school. I was quickly enrolled there, on the understanding that I would leave at fifteen to take my 'O' levels at the Chester College of Further Education.

Life at this country school was a refreshing new experience for me and there were girls there too. I had not been used to relating to women since my early childhood, when I had a few girl friends. However, until the age of seven or eight I can clearly remember wishing I could be a woman (especially when I had crushes on male film stars!). Later these feelings seemed to evaporate, as did an interest in feminine things. I became just like all the other boys and enjoyed playing with cars, trains and planes.

I soon felt very much at home in this school. For the first time in my school career I was near the top of the class, mainly because of my past education. The emphasis on sport was not as strong, although even I was able to show them how to play rugger. In many ways I seemed to be respected and accepted, partly because of my grand home and school background. It was also at this time that I became aware of a sexual interest or curiosity in some of the other boys, rather than just emotional feelings. In the public school we were used to one another's bodies, as we bathed and showered together. However, these boys were much more modest and shy as far as their bodies were concerned and this made me feel the same way. Perhaps this accounted for the sexual curiosity that developed in me and, possibly, in one or two of them.

After about eighteen months, the time came for me to move to college in Chester for my 'O' levels.

One of the understandings, when we moved to the farm, was that my father would not have to work as hard at the bakery business in Liverpool. Sadly, this arrangement had not worked out and he made the difficult journey every day. This became a strain on him and a worry for my mother so reluctantly it was decided that we should move back to Liverpool and a house was bought. I then began commuting to college in Chester from Liverpool.

College life was far less disciplined than school and it was not long before I began to take advantage of this. If I missed my train in the morning I would spend the day wandering around Birkenhead or Liverpool, arriving home at the normal time. My sexuality was certainly developing now and I knew I was definitely interested in men. However, I found it difficult to believe that they would be interested in me until I was older, because at sixteen my voice had still not broken. A fascination with the male physique encouraged me to start buying bodybuilding magazines, which were supposedly for athletic interest, but I think were really produced for homosexuals. They were the equivalent of 'girlie' magazines. This was before the days of blatant homosexual pornography but, nevertheless, interest in these magazines soon became something of an addiction. I used to hide them at home, but I know my mother discovered them at various times, although nothing was ever said. I guess she must have been very concerned, but possibly thought it was part of my 'growing up process' – this was the early 'swinging sixties'. It was at this time that I discovered a place in Liverpool, near my bus stop, where homosexuals met for sexual relationships. There was no social contact, it was simply a place for importuning. I was fascinated, but too shy to get involved. I found myself frequently drawn back to this place and others I soon discovered, but never plucked up enough courage to 'go off' with anyone.

I had an active imagination and at this time used to pretend I was a famous singer, with lots of money, buying Rolls Royces and large houses for my family and myself. A lot of this had developed because of my brother's theatrical influence – I had been taken backstage since I was seven and had met several famous people. The major problem was that I was so shy I would hardly ever speak to anyone, unless spoken to, and my fantasy world seemed very unlikely ever to become reality. Perhaps it was the extrovert within seeking to break out! I remember once overhearing my father talking to one of the teachers from the secondary modern school, saying, 'I'm worried about Martin, he doesn't seem to have anything about him!' I think this would have been the general impression given by my quiet, shy nature. I never used to swear or blaspheme and had a vague idea about God's existence. I used to pray every night, just in case he was there somewhere. I also avoided walking under ladders, kept my fingers crossed and read the horoscopes – to keep all the options open! I wanted good things to come my way. I had been to Crusader classes in Liverpool many years earlier and even went to a big celebration with them at the Albert Hall in London. However, the spiritual content and teaching must have gone straight over my head, because the only thing I can remember is looking at the torn and tattered curtains on the stage of the community hall where we met and wanting to rearrange them, so that they would look more theatrically aesthetic! This is no reflection on the Crusader class. The leaders were warm and caring but somehow the teaching did not penetrate my brain. My parents were saying, 'We must go to church more often', but they never did and it remained a resolution that only really bore fruit after I became a Christian myself, twelve years later.

It was not surprising that I failed all my 'O' levels and father felt I should go away to college in Blackpool to get some qualifications for the bakery business. Then at least I would have something to show for all my schooling. I agreed and was soon lodging in a homely boarding house in Blackpool with two other students from the College of Food Technology. They were in the Hotel and Catering Department and I was in the Bakery College.

Before long I began to get very emotionally involved with one of my fellow lodgers, Simon, and we became very close friends. He was a gentle and sensitive person. I longed to share my feelings with him, but was too scared. I wondered if maybe he felt the same way. Could he have homosexual feelings as well?

One day, I decided to take the plunge and wrote him a note explaining something of my feelings, without using words like 'homosexual'. I still refused to use that kind of identity, although I frequently felt myself blushing if the word was mentioned, or expressions like 'queer' or 'fairy' were used in conversation. The note was left in Simon's bedroom with a copy of a male photo magazine called *The Young Physique*. It was fairly cryptic and simply said, 'I think you ought to know that I am interested in this kind of thing . . .' I was of course hoping that he was as well. Simon did not come running along to me with open arms and say, 'Martin, I feel like this too!' His reaction was not really what I expected. He said that he did not mind me feeling like this, but if I was to continue as his friend, then others must not know about me, in case they suspected that he might be a 'queer'. He warned me about the way one or two others in the college like that were ostracised. He advised me to watch the way I walked and sat down. That is, not with legs tightly crossed, in an 'effeminate manner', but with both feet firmly on the floor, knees wide apart! Simon's fears were accentuated because some more students from his department were about to move in the next day. The following evening I worked really hard on the 'macho' image. I managed to stop crossing my legs all evening and was surprised how easy it seemed to be. Simon came up to me later and said in a very affirming manner, 'Martin you managed really well. Keep it up!'

Simon and the new lodgers, Gavin and Tony, were always talking about their female conquests. Simon was obviously the least experienced and somewhat in awe of the other two, with a childlike admiration. One evening a trip to the cinema was arranged and a girlfriend allocated for me. This was not the first time I had taken out a girl. I had shown a little interest in a girl at the secondary school, but nothing had really developed in the way of a relationship. At that time I was to some extent hoping to prove to myself that I was 'normal', but now it was probably just an attempt to be accepted by Simon and his friends.

I was determined to prove myself and had nearly every move carefully planned, although it really seemed like an ordeal. Before very long I took the plunge and put my arm around Susan's shoulder. She moved her head towards mine and I was predominantly aware of her false eyelashes tickling my cheekbone. I could not concentrate on any of the film (a two-and-a-half-hour epic) because of my self-consciousness and concern about my next move. I did not enjoy the experience at all, but it served a very important purpose for me. I was now much more accepted and trusted by the others. Simon came to me afterwards with a look of admiration on his face and said, 'You were all right there! – I saw you – you didn't waste any time, did you? You were the first to make a move! I was really proud of you.' He also made a point of exclaiming to the others, 'Did you see Martin – eh! There's nothing wrong with him is there?'

I soon discovered to my horror that Susan was known as easily available for sex and what was even worse, she fancied me! I managed to convince the others that I did not really like her type anyway and avoided any other 'heavy' relationships with women, whilst still keeping Gavin and Tony 'off the scent'. Many times I would be alone with Simon in the car and long for his affection. We frequently drove to my home in Liverpool or his in Northumberland, for a few days together. The nearest my dream ever came to reality was when on a long overnight coach journey from Blackpool to London, he fell asleep and his head, probably accidentally, fell onto my shoulder. It felt wonderful, even though I was a little self-conscious.

After two very happy years in Blackpool, I moved back to Liverpool to work in the family bakery business. I now had my only academic qualification, a National Bakery Diploma. I still knew no one else with homosexual feelings.

2
A New Lifestyle

Back in Liverpool, only a couple of my friends had not moved on to university or college. A few were still in Chester, but it was too far just to drop in and see them. By this time, I had my own car, a Volkswagen, and, at a loose end, began to drift towards the places of sexual interest I had discovered on my way home from school. While at Blackpool, my voice had broken. I was eighteen at the time and now felt more confident that I was old enough to be sexually attractive to another man. I started meeting people in these sexual cruising places, but still had no sex or even social contact with them. We would just agree there was nowhere to go for sex and I would disappear. I was still very nervous.

Then, one weekend, my parents had gone away and I had the house to myself. I went out cruising for the evening and met a guy called Hans, who claimed to be German, and took him home. He was about 28 and a rather mysterious character. I found him very attractive indeed. After our encounter I longed to meet up with him again. I realised I did not have his address or phone number so several times went out to search for him, which made him even more exciting. He had a distinctive old Mercedes limousine, so whenever I spotted it there was an adrenaline rush. By this stage I had experienced a few brief sexual encounters, but I never met anyone I wanted to see again, or who was as exciting as Hans.

Eventually I tracked Hans down again, and he revealed to me that he was not in fact German but an English schoolteacher and his name was Geoff. He was involved with another man called John. Geoff eventually asked me if I had ever been inside 'one of the 'gay pubs' in Liverpool'. I said 'No', but felt curious to see what they were like. I was very nervous and hesitant to go into one of these places on my own. However, one night I plucked up the courage and was surprised to see how well appointed the pub seemed to be. It was called The Magic Clock and when I looked around I spotted Geoff and his friend John, sitting in a corner. The pub was full of people and had a man in his fifties with a white coat and a pronounced limp standing by the door, as if on guard. In fact, I soon learned that his job was to look out for any potential trouble-makers and keep them out.

I got to know Geoff quite well and used to drive him and John around. We had an almost daily routine. Geoff would meet John in town and go to The Magic Clock. Then I would arrive at about 9.30 or 10pm, have a drink with them and sometimes one or two others. We would leave in my car, with Geoff and John holding hands in the back seat. After we had dropped John off, I would drive Geoff home and we would usually have some sort of sex play in the car together. We also used to talk for hours. Sometimes I would not arrive home until 3am. Considering I was up for work at 5am, it meant I soon became very run-down physically. I used to convince my father that I was not tired and encouraged my parents to believe that I had not been all that late coming home. I kept myself going with caffeine tablets, strong coffee and a long rest in the afternoon, after work. I went to bed between 3 and 4 o'clock in the afternoon, got up at about 7 or 7.30 in the evening, dressed and went down to the pub at 9. Occasionally, when not with Geoff and John, I would get involved in other sexual relationships. My strong sexual feelings for Geoff, however, had grown into a very deep emotional attachment. My parents met Geoff and John, plus one or two other friends I had made from the pub. At this stage, I was trying to convince them it was really a coffee bar I was visiting.

Geoff was not really attracted to me sexually, even though I knew I could arouse him. In turn I started to meet a few more people who showed a lot of interest in me sexually, but I was not really attracted to them; in fact I never met anyone else as attractive to me as Geoff. John knew about my feelings and relationship with Geoff, but it did not seem to bother him. He showed very little real emotional interest in Geoff. How I longed to be loved by Geoff, as much as he loved John.

I now spent very little time with any of my friends who were not homosexual. Most of them were no longer in the area, anyway. The only sense of real duplicity I felt was in my secrecy at home and also at work. I wanted to be accepted by the workers in the bakehouse and started swearing, blaspheming and telling obscene jokes. They thought, as far as I know, that I was a womaniser. They called me

A New Lifestyle

'the Whoremaster'. There were times when jokes were made about 'queers' and my heart would miss a beat. Sometimes they told me I should go down to The Magic Clock 'for a laugh at the queers'. I smiled uneasily. Occasionally I worried in case I bumped into any of the bakehouse staff in the pub, but tried to keep a convincing story in my mind, just in case I was spotted. I knew the doorman was very careful about letting 'sightseers' into the pub.

I still said my prayers, believe it or not, but in very much the same attitude of mind as before. If, sometimes, I had a twinge of conscience, I would overcome it by saying, 'Oh I'm sure God doesn't mind'. I used to pray that I would meet attractive people and then use a few other prayers hopefully to make it sound religiously good. Having said that, I never really thought about God at all seriously. As before, it was as if he was a sort of 'good luck charm' for me to try, along with anything else in the same realm.

Occasionally, I travelled to a club in Manchester and on one occasion met someone called Tony. He was quite good looking, but without Geoff's athletic physique, and I was not aware of a strong sexual attraction for him. Despite this, Tony made it clear that he was very interested in me and I started to develop a relationship with him. Tony was a romantic and would often write poems to me and send love letters. It was nice to feel wanted and needed. We were always together at parties and in the pub. We went on a short holiday, staying in a hotel in Wales. It was all a new experience for me. Tony's mother encouraged the relationship and loved to make sure we were tucked up safely in bed together. This was because he had been fairly promiscuous and often brought people home for a 'one-night stand'. Now, it seemed he wanted to be faithful to me. I enjoyed the romance and the sense of belonging to someone, but I still had much stronger feelings for Geoff, whom I was still seeing.

Tony got a job at the Magic Clock as a barman and I knew that my parents would have to know something, by this time. I was often staying away from home at weekends while I was with Tony. Then came my twenty-first birthday party and I would be expected to invite many of my friends to this. I told my parents that Tony was working at a pub in town called The Magic Clock, and explained that it used to have a reputation, but was now owned by a respected catering firm that my parents knew well. This was in fact true, because this firm had thought at one time of opening it as an 'up-market' restaurant. I think I managed, to some extent, to pull the wool over their eyes. My parents had experienced a lot of worry because of my brother's psychological and personality problems and it concerned me that they might think my life was going in the same direction.

I took my relationship with Tony very much for granted and I guess really used him to satisfy my own ego and need to feel wanted. It was good to go to parties with a partner and not appear alone. There was a sense in which I was proud to 'belong' to someone and show others that I was worth something to someone else. It is difficult to describe the sense of comfort and security this brings, but I am sure it is comparable to a heterosexual boyfriend and girlfriend relationship. At that point it was these feelings of security, which seemed more apparent than any sense of 'being in love' with Tony.

One evening a friend said to me, 'Martin, you know unless you change your attitude to Tony and respond to him more, you will lose him. You can't keep holding up a candle to Geoff for ever.' This really struck home and over the next day I chewed over the implications of all he said to me. I realised that now I was very frightened of losing Tony. He meant more to me than I thought and I started to panic, making moves to ensure the stability of our relationship. The first step was to buy him a very attractive ring from Liverpool's best jeweller. This meant a lot to him but did not prevent the inevitable change in our relationship. Because Tony now felt secure with me he began flirting with other people. This was not very difficult as he worked behind the bar of The Magic Clock, where a high percentage of the customers showed some sexual interest in him. At times I would arrive late at the pub and know for sure that he had been involved sexually with someone else. He would usually get slightly drunk before he could face me, but then it almost seemed as if he wanted me to know about his unfaithfulness, and had a strange sadistic desire to hurt. He would deliberately introduce me to his sex partner, with a very 'knowing' look on his face as if the two of them had a secret they did not want me to share. My stomach would turn over in the pain of fear, insecurity and jealousy. Then Tony would try to make it up to me by playing sentimental songs over the pub's music system, often in tears to prove I was the only one who really mattered to him. One of his favourites was Cilla Black's 'You're My World', which he said was just for me. On occasions he would temporarily reject me until he sobered up. Whatever

A New Lifestyle

happened, it was a very painful experience, with which anyone having an unfaithful lover can identify.

One of the most difficult situations I experienced with Tony was when on holiday in Majorca. I wanted us both to steer clear of any homosexual company, because of the threat of Tony's unfaithfulness. However, inevitably, Tony persuaded me to go into the homosexual bars with him. At first there were no problems and we also mixed socially with some of the married couples on the package holiday, which pleased me, of course. One evening, Tony was a little drunk and met a guy he wanted. This person's friend wanted me, and Tony thought this was a great idea. As far as I was concerned it was certainly not on! Tony got angry and tried to bring his guy into our hotel room. Amazingly, I plucked up enough courage to persuade the hotel porter to ask the stranger to leave. I was only wearing my briefs at the time, but the strong emotions stifled any embarrassment. The guy Tony picked up said, 'Martin, your relationship won't last on the gay scene, if you're not prepared to give Tony some freedom to have sex with others.' I said, 'I'm not prepared to do that!' For the rest of the holiday, Tony decided to ignore me. It was a very difficult and traumatic experience; in fact every time I went anywhere near those homosexual bars, the hurt made my stomach turn over.

We noticed another person in the hotel, whom we suspected of being gay. Tony occasionally spoke to him, but because of my determination to avoid anyone else like that, in case Tony wanted him, he was ignored by me. He was obviously from our area, because he flew with us from Liverpool Airport. A few weeks later, on our return home, this person appeared in The Magic Clock and came over to speak to me. He simply said he had seen the situation between Tony and me on holiday and wanted me to know that he was disgusted at the way I had been treated. He introduced himself as John and said, 'You deserve better than that. Why do you hang around a place like this? If you ever want to get away, come over to my place in Southport.' After a lot of tears, Tony and I parted company. It was the first time I had cried for many years. Despite all the hurt, I did not want us to part.

I took John up on his invitation and met a whole new circle of friends. They were all gay, but did not spend much time in the pubs and clubs. Many had really beautiful houses and we often had dinner parties, went to the theatre and holidayed together.

Ironically, a few months after we parted I met Tony one evening and he asked me to give him a lift home. He wanted us to sleep together – 'for old time's sake' and I agreed. It seemed as if he might have thoughts of rekindling our relationship. I was astonished at my reaction: a few months earlier it would have been the answer to my prayers. Now I felt quite differently and almost cold in my emotional response to him. I did not want the hurt and insecurity I experienced before. Time had healed a lot of the hurt – but, as I discovered years later, not all.

Within this new circle of friends, there were six of us who were especially close. Some had stable relationships, having been together for many years. They seemed very much to me like married couples. They had set up home together and very rarely went into a gay pub or club. This was to avoid sexual temptation or unfaithfulness.

Many of the couples that had been together for a long time had an arrangement whereby one partner would be allowed to go off occasionally for another sexual encounter. However, social involvement in these sexual situations was rare, because any emotional attachment would present a threat to the stability of these long-term relationships.

I was fairly promiscuous, although I was, ideally, really longing for a more lasting and stable relationship. With this underlying desire at the back of my mind, sex was something of a hobby. My friends and I frequently shared stories of our sexual encounters. Provided no one was hurt and an existing relationship was not harmed in any way, we had no strong conviction that this way of life was wrong. There was a tremendous sense of loyalty between us. For example, if I became emotionally involved with someone and the relationship did not work out, my friends would contact me to see if I was all right. They would invite me round, or call, to make sure I was coping. By this time I was buying my own house and lived alone for most of the time. One of my close circle of friends, Richard, lived only a few miles away, but the others were about three-quarters of an hour's drive into Lancashire. Richard was probably over twenty years older than me, but we never really thought much about the age difference. He was very much the 'English country gentleman' and, although our family backgrounds were very different, we enjoyed one another's company. He was very houseproud and always repairing and decorating. He helped

A New Lifestyle

me in many practical ways in my own home. We often went to the theatre and concerts together and sometimes to places where we thought we might make 'a sexual pick-up', but there was no sexual involvement between us. I missed Richard when his job took him to Birmingham. However, my other friends did not allow me to get too lonely, even though they were quite a distance away. From time to time we would meet new people, either through a local club or a mutual friend.

My social life was therefore quite fulfilling. Mother and father were now much more involved with my friends than ever before. They liked them very much and my friends accepted them in turn. I had still not told my parents about my homosexuality, and although I guessed they probably knew, it still seemed something of a difficult subject to talk to them about. I wanted to make it clear that my gay lifestyle was different and much more 'normal and acceptable' than my brother's. It was all unspoken, but I assumed they knew most of what was going on in my life and accepted it.

My lifestyle could be compared to some extent with many heterosexuals: enjoying an active social life, but always on the look-out for an attractive person who would be a 'good catch'! This, however, was not as apparent as in some parts of the homosexual community, where one can see a real 'rat race' to compete against one another in the 'sexual stakes'. The desire to be attractive can become an all-consuming form of self-idolatry, even though it never really works in the long term. It rarely convinces the person concerned and, in my experience, often drives others away. I guess it is fear and insecurity in one person reacting with similar issues in another. I found the long-lasting homosexual relationships were ones in which the two people involved were different in many ways. They complemented one another, rather than competing or trying to be as physically attractive as each other. One of my major problems in forming a lasting homosexual relationship was that I felt I needed a 'masculine' type of partner, whereas the majority of people who were attracted to me were seeing in my physical appearance just such a 'masculine' image – not what I felt inside. I guess I looked for strengths (physical and emotional) in others, which I desired for myself.

Many of those I met had a deep concern for others and a high standard of 'moral' behaviour, even though I was to learn later that this was not really in accord with Christian standards. For example, if someone was involved in a sexual relationship and did not want to become deeply emotional, he would make that clear to his sexual partner and possibly even break off the relationship. This was so that the other person involved would not get hurt. This was certainly part of my experience. I was nearly always treated with compassion and respect, even though it meant I could not have the person I wanted. On one occasion I met an architect who was very into black and white in design. This was true of his clothes and his black car. We were involved sexually and I wanted more from the relationship. He was fearful of getting involved again, following the recent break-up of a relationship. I decided to play it cool, but make sure I was available if he should change his mind. I bought black trousers and jumper. My friends joked about it – calling me 'The Black Widow'. One night I spotted this man in the club with a black guy. A friend said, 'Now what are you going to do Martin?' I gave up the chase!

Discretion was also a keynote within my own circle of friends. We would often meet quite well-known public figures, especially from the world of entertainment. We never talked about their homosexuality, or even mentioned that we had met, in case it caused them problems. We were not into 'outing' people in those days.

I was popular with my friends and there was a very deep sense of love, commitment and therefore loyalty between us. We were not in any way flaunting our homosexuality. In fact at times, especially with relatives and friends who did not know about us, we revelled in the 'undercover secrecy' – the knowing glance to each other, when in so-called 'straight' company, and the use of a language partly from the theatrical world, which was at this time just becoming more generally known. Words such as 'gay', 'camp', 'drag', 'naff' and many others could be used quite often with a double meaning. This all helped us to take life and ourselves far less seriously than perhaps we might have done. It has often been said that the use of the word 'gay' is a lie when referring to homosexuality, but I would have disagreed because in my situation, at that time I would have said there was much gaiety, as in the original meaning of the word. I had developed a lifestyle that was fulfilling and pleasant for me and for my close friends. It was selfish and self-centred in some ways. We did very little to help others, or the world in which we lived, although I must stress that is far from being the

A New Lifestyle

case with other people in the homosexual community. I know many who work very hard for the good of others in self-sacrificing ways.

What reason did I have to believe that my secure little world was not what God wanted for me? None, as far as I could see: I had good friends, a happy social life, a good home and car, plus a secure job. It would have been nice to be the famous singer and performer of my fantasies, but I was living in the real world now and it was pretty good. There was one gap in my life that I really longed to be filled. I wanted a lover to whom I was attracted and with whom I could live and share my life. I had already seen something of that with my friends, but somehow it never really worked out for me. Deep down I realised that I set my standards far too high and was reaching for the impossible, but still that hope lay not too far beneath my consciousness. It was my prayer to a God whom I hoped might be there and bring such a 'knight in shining armour' into my life.

I had a reputation for holding good parties, especially when they were fancy dress. It was great fun making the costumes for those who did not hire Roman centurions or Regency buffs from the theatrical costumiers. It was also an opportunity to make new friends, as guests were often brought along. One such person was Ken. He was from London, tall, slim and obviously quite an extrovert. There was, however, a sense in which I felt Ken was holding back. He was not the sort of 'high-powered London queen' I would have expected him to be. They usually tried to impress with all that was happening in London's large homosexual subculture and often made us northerners feel we are about twenty years behind their development and sophistication. I guess it may be a bit different these days, with places like the 'Gay Village' in Manchester. Ken apparently knew we would see him as possibly arrogant and therefore kept quietly in the background. He actually preferred our way of life in the north, feeling it was much more genuine and less pressurised than the London scene. This was the same person who once unknowingly tapped on Prince Charles's shoulder in the Royal Opera House and growled, 'Will you please be quiet!', then felt awful when he recognised the Prince, who incidentally was very gracious and apologetic. He was thinking seriously of giving up a very lucrative job in London and moving to Merseyside to work as a poorly paid technician in a local hospital. His only reservation was that he would miss the opera at Covent Garden (a major love of his life). Ken eventually moved to Merseyside and I began to know him quite well.

Many of my friends had to give me a heavy push when it came to meeting others socially, with a view to a relationship. I was very shy and found it almost impossible to take the initiative when in a pub or club. One evening, Ken came up to me with a rather shy but nice-looking man. He was not physically tall and overpowering, which I normally found attractive, but there was something nice about him. Ken said, 'Martin, I want you to meet Tim.' Then, with a twinkle in his eye, because he knew it would appeal, added, 'Tim is a rugby player.' We started talking and it seemed clear that Ken had met Tim the night before and been to bed with him. Tim did not stay very long, but said he would see me in there again. He seemed very shy and not used to a gay environment. Later Ken asked if I liked him and said he would 'see what he could do for me'. He obviously liked him as well, so his offer seemed very unselfish. He did point out that Tim was very new to all this and therefore needed a lot of encouragement. I decided I would really like to meet him again.

3
A New Friend

THE BONAPARTE WAS THE NAME of the club in which I had been introduced to Tim. There are several impressive and listed buildings in the business section of Liverpool city centre which had rooms leased for private parties. The rooms that formed the Bonaparte were licensed, but rented by the people running it. One evening at about 9.30 I arrived to find Tim there on his own. With some hesitation, in case he didn't want to see me, I walked over to him. 'Hello, can I join you?' I said nervously. 'Yes, let me get you a drink' he replied in what my brother used to call a 'South Kensington Accent'. He sounded to me a bit like someone from the Royal Family! Luckily Richard, the friend who moved to Birmingham, also had a similarly 'posh' voice and an eccentric flamboyant manner to go with it, so some of my inferiority complexes had already been overcome in that relationship. Tim's manner was so gentle, shy and loving that my nervousness was slowly being overcome. It seemed he had recently moved to Birkenhead, near Liverpool, in his job as a trainee manager. A few weeks before, while living near Preston, he met another homosexual, also from Liverpool. They had a sexual relationship, but it was the first time Tim had experienced anything like it or met another homosexual socially. He was hurting inside quite a bit. 'I really don't know if this is the sort of life I want', he said. 'It's all very strange to me.' I tried to assure him that before long it would all seem quite natural and normal.

The first time I went to a homosexual party I remember feeling it was all very strange, but that soon changed when I became used to the environment. Tim didn't seem totally convinced as I shared my experience with him, but I felt determined to prove to him how right I was. He didn't wait for the club to close before leaving to catch the river ferry to Birkenhead. A couple of nights later he was in the Bonaparte again and I asked him, along with a few others, to come to my place for coffee. He agreed and seemed a bit more willing to talk.

When we were apart from the others in our group, it seemed easier to talk and he told me that he really had been 'smitten' by this man in Preston and was finding it difficult to recover from his feelings of hurt. I tried to convince him that I could identify with his experience, and I wanted to offer help and comfort. Then Tim said, 'Martin, I know you will think this sounds silly, but I'm really not at all sure that this way of life is right. You see I am a Christian.' I was quite touched by what I thought was his naivety. I said, 'Well I'm a Christian too, but I'm sure it's OK. They do say all sorts of leading clergymen are gay and pick up people for sex. I honestly wouldn't worry about that.' I told him of a bishop I'd heard about, who picked up men on the M6. Tim didn't seem impressed at all. He was obviously not convinced. I decided to take him under my wing and show him how much he could enjoy being gay. I would introduce him to my closest friends. After all, his experience of the homosexual lifestyle was very limited indeed. It also seemed clear to me that I must not make any strong moves towards him myself, in case it frightened him off. I really didn't know whether he was interested in me or not. He was obviously in a very delicate state emotionally and not ready for another relationship just yet. I decided to follow the advice my friends had so often given me before and 'play it cool' with him. I was living in hope, though.

There was something very appealing about this guy Tim who called himself a Christian. He was also good looking and fit, which attracted me even more. We had a pleasant but quiet evening with some friends in my house. Tim seemed a bit more relaxed at my home and said he had never met anyone living alone in their own house like that before. Apparently his parents didn't know anything about his homosexuality, neither did his sister, Jane, or brother-in-law, Andrew, whom he said were also Christians. He was very close to them and would like them to know about himself, one day. It was actually his ambition to be married and have a family. 'I love children', he said, 'and, besides, all my school chums are getting married . . . with all the excitement and preparations, it just makes me long for it myself.' That was a feeling and desire I could not pretend to share or really appreciate.

I decided to have a party, so I could help Tim see how much fun there was for him in our type of lifestyle. It was to be one of my fancy dress parties and I invited all the friends I knew who would make it go with a swing, especially two from Manchester. They both used to perform and mime Judy Garland, Liza Minnelli or Marlene Dietrich records, but only when sufficiently drunk. They hardly had an ounce of rhythm in their bodies, but it was so funny I used to be quite sore with laughter – probably because I knew them so well and it was such a contrast to their 'respectable image'. Before this party I was able to spend quite a bit of time getting to know Tim. He said little more about his Christian beliefs, but I sensed he was holding back in some way. There seemed to be a sincerity and simplicity there that was quite different from other 'religious' people I had met. My brother had been converted to Roman Catholicism about eight years earlier and the conversations that he and his friends had about religion were almost completely incomprehensible to me. It just seemed like another brand of intellectualism. Also my brother, being very prone to melodrama, became totally obsessed with the altar he made in his bedroom, filling the house with the fumes of the incense he continually burned. His friends, the priests, told my parents that his long religious rituals were quite unnecessary.

At this time my relationship with my brother was not at all good. I think I probably hated him, because of all the hurt and upset he brought to my parents through heavy drinking and extravagant living. Hence I found it very difficult to take his religion at all seriously. It was one facet of his lifestyle that alienated him from me. I was no longer as impressed as I had been by the flamboyance of his theatrical world. I rarely stopped to think that my parents could have been also worried about *my* lifestyle! Certainly it became clear later that my attitude to my brother worried my mother a lot. She never really showed her deepest feelings and anxieties and at that time I often wondered if she had any, apart from the obvious ones concerning my brother. Having said that, my mother's inner tensions had caused two heart attacks; I therefore later tried to ensure there were as few anxieties in her life as possible.

The other religious people I had met were very 'straight-laced', non-drinking and serious people. At least that is the way I viewed them then. Later my impression changed considerably.

So my idea of Christian people was that some were rather dull and boring (although I had a sneaking respect for them) while others seemed to be trying desperately to prove to people like me how ordinary and normal they were. They drank, smoked, swore and did not even seem too bothered about sexual promiscuity. Tim was therefore very different from anyone else I had met before who claimed to have a faith in God.

The plans for the party were slightly changed in that it was decided it would not be fancy dress. There really was not enough time to prepare for this and in any case I thought Tim would probably find it more difficult to cope with.

As the party got under way, Tim seemed fairly relaxed and at home. By this time he had begun to know quite a few of the people there and was making friendly conversation with some and able to joke with others. Normally, at these parties we would drink as much as was available. Certainly I found it always helped my self-confidence to have a drink continually in my hand. Because I felt Tim was probably even more shy and timid in this situation than he was normally, I tried to make sure his glass was always being filled, but was surprised by the fact that he frequently refused more drink. I knew in his situation I would have needed it to boost my self-confidence. I desperately wanted Tim to experience the enjoyment I felt at these events, especially when I managed to persuade my friends from Manchester to perform for us. It took a lot of careful planning and plenty of alcohol to bring them to the point of doing their 'turn'. They really enjoyed themselves and, as usual, I was convulsed in laughter, but Tim did not seem tremendously impressed, only a little amused. The party ended, with most of us feeling it had been a success, and Tim drove a few people home. He had enjoyed himself, while remaining completely sober, but I felt there had been little development in our relationship.

A few weeks went by with no change in the situation. I was now beginning to feel much more strongly that I wanted a very special relationship with Tim, but for some reason it seemed much more of an emotional desire rather than a sexual one. I had not made any sexual advances towards him, nor was I burning up with a lust to do so. It may have been because I doubted that Tim was interested in me sexually, although I didn't know for sure that this was true. Eventually I asked him to the theatre for my birthday, and he accepted. The day before our trip I was feeling particularly low and discouraged as far as this new relationship was concerned. I had not really given any thought to Tim's religious beliefs, and in fact he said very little more about them. At about 9 o'clock I decided to go

A New Friend

out for a drink to cheer myself up. Instead of making my usual trip to Liverpool, I went to Chester for a change. At that time the gay bar in Chester was part of a smart hotel in the centre of town. I met a couple of acquaintances there and one guy seemed quite keen for me to go back to his place. I declined his offer and decided to make my own way home alone. While driving down a country road on that chilly March evening I felt a wave of depression hit me. I thought to myself, 'What on earth am I doing with my life? Where's it going?' Thoughts of Tim came into my mind. I was in love once more. I said, 'Oh God, why is this happening all over again?' Thoughts of many experiences of unrequited love came to mind . . . 'Oh God, not again!'

Immediately a voice within seemed to say, 'Don't worry, Martin. I have brought Tim into your life . . . for you!'

I was stunned. 'Was that God speaking – or me?' I felt a strange sense of peace within and real hope. I decided to continue seeking to relate to Tim. I wanted to throw out any doubts that lingered, in case God really had spoken to me. There was a new-found joy in my heart, but after a while another thought suddenly struck me. 'If that really was God, I'd better try to be good – try to know more about him – otherwise he could change his mind and take Tim away!' I arrived home and went to bed with an instinctive feeling that this was a new beginning in my life.

The next morning, my birthday, I went to work in a rather subdued mood. I was not sure just how to react to what happened in the car the night before, but I sensed a kind of 'presence' with me and a peace within. I was still a bit suspicious, in case it was just all part of my imagination, spurred on by wishful thinking. That afternoon, after work, I decided to make a step towards God and thought I would read the Bible. It was not difficult to find a Bible my uncle had given me when I was christened. It had remained on the bookshelf, almost untouched, for many years. I can remember looking through it a few times when I was a child and liking the rich colourful pictures on glossy paper. It always seemed to have a very special smell, slightly sweet and certainly different from any other book – probably the leather binding. I started to read the Gospel according to St Matthew, which seemed a logical place to begin in the New Testament. I loved my recording of *Jesus Christ Superstar* and had just seen an Italian film, *The Gospel of St Matthew*. I started to read, 'The book of the generation of Jesus

Christ, the son of David, the son . . .' This really was a new experience for me, but there was something very challenging and exciting about it. In a way, the archaic language of the Authorised Version added to the mystique of this new experience. Somehow the words and their sense were not as difficult to understand as I had always imagined. There was certainly something very special about this book. I wasn't an avid reader of any books, which made my desire to read my Bible even more surprising.

I had a very pleasant evening with Tim and he bought me a tie for my birthday, which meant a lot to me. I said nothing of my experience the night before, but mentioned I had started reading the Bible. Then Tim told me, with some hesitation, that he wanted to see someone about his homosexuality. I was still puzzled by his reaction to sexuality. I didn't want to say too much about my own thoughts, as far as God was concerned, until I could understand them myself. I was a bit wary of him thinking I wanted to encourage him or move too quickly in the relationship. Again and again, my friends had warned me to 'play it cool'.

The next step I decided to take, in trying to please God, was to go to church. This was a mighty and difficult task for me to undertake. I made up my mind to go in the evening, so I would not have to go home for lunch (as I did, nearly every Sunday) afterwards. How could I ever explain this to my parents, let alone my friends? That evening I put on my best suit and made my way into the little village church, near where I lived. I just hoped that no one would speak to me. I wanted to give the impression that I was a seasoned churchgoer and knew all the right things to do. They must not know that I couldn't find my way around the 1662 prayer book.

Once in the ancient pew of this old parish church, my apprehension and self-consciousness erupted in the form of a heavy sweat. How embarrassed I was! I managed the prayer book fairly well, although once or twice, when I was a little lost, the woman next to me smiled and showed me the place. I was not aware of fumbling for long enough to make her suspicious, but my newness to this environment must have shown. I wanted to rush out as inconspicuously as possible, hoping that no one would say anything to me. There were about 25 people in the neat and fairly plain old church building and they all seemed to know each other. The vicar was busy talking to people as they left. He glanced over to me and looked as if he would rush towards me, through the people around

A New Friend

him, if I lingered at all. I made him be content with a glance and the words, 'Nice to see you here!' I nodded and beat a hasty retreat.

I later told Tim I had been to church, but without admitting the difficulties involved in the process. He began to ask if it was a church where the Gospel was preached and then explained what he meant by that. He told me how he became a Christian while at school. I often used to hear, in our own school chapel, that Christ died for our sins, though what that actually meant had never been formalised or worked out in my brain. It was just words. As Tim gently shared his own experiences with me, it all made so much more sense than ever before. The idea of sin separating me from God, and Jesus as the perfect sacrifice for that sin, was something I could begin to understand and accept, rather than the complex phraseology of the formal prayers in school. Underlining this new-found understanding of the Gospel was the fact that I was beginning to understand something of the perfect humanity of Jesus, through reading Matthew's Gospel. The personality that really shone through the pages to me was one of a perfect man. He seemed to lack any fear, prejudice, anger or other human traits that I had assumed were quite normal. These very special qualities of Jesus made me realise that he really is God and also encouraged me to pay very close attention to all that he was teaching through the Gospel account.

I found that the inner voice that spoke to me on that journey home from Chester was now a constant companion. Sometimes in the bakery I would experience God's presence in unexpected ways. For example, my hand would pull away seconds before some boiling jam was spilt. It could not have been a reflex action because it happened before the jam spilt, not at the same time, or after. On other occasions I would be packing some fancy cakes and pick up a handful of cases for them. Many, many times there were exactly the right amount – no more no less. On all these occasions the inner voice just gently said, 'You see, it's going to be all right, everything will work out.' Each time I felt a sense of real assurance and peace.

Tim left a booklet with me called *Journey Into Life*. This was a simple and straightforward account of the Gospel and how to become a Christian. It was well illustrated with helpful diagrams and ended with the prayer of commitment. It seemed to relate very much to all I had been experiencing of God and had learned from Tim. I thought I made some kind of decision or choice to follow

Christ on my way home from Chester, but prayed the prayer of commitment in the book just to be doubly sure. I continued to go to the local church and although the vicar did sometimes mention something of a personal relationship with Jesus, rather than the religious intellectualism I heard before, he seemed a bit vague and disillusioned. In almost every sermon he asked us to consider giving more money towards church repairs. I sensed very much that he was fighting a lonely battle.

Tim phoned one day to say he had arranged to see a vicar of a church in Wirral, called Roy Barker. 'I have prayed that God will speak to me through him, on this whole question of my homosexuality. Will you pray for me too?' I agreed, with some apprehension.

'How did you get on Tim?' I asked, when he phoned a couple of hours later.

'Very well. I'm sure our prayers were answered. Roy really seemed to understand what I was talking about. He has come across it before. He said, "Tim, I know some people will tell you differently, but I'm sorry I feel I have to say that scripture clearly says homosexual practice is wrong. It doesn't condemn you for having a homosexual orientation and temptations."' Tim continued, 'He showed me where this is mentioned in scripture and I do feel at peace about it now. I am sure he is right, you know. You and I prayed that God would speak through him and I feel that has happened.'

'I'm not sure, Tim', I said. 'Why should God say it's wrong?'

'Because God intends sex to be only within marriage, between a man and woman.'

'But why should we have these feelings if they're not right?' I asked.

'I don't know, but I do believe that God can give me the power to overcome them and maybe even take them away. I'd love to be able to get married and have a family, one day.'

'Well, I guess he may be right, but I would have thought if two men love each other . . .' I said, rather unconvinced.

'I really must start going to his church', Tim said; 'I've heard quite a bit about it. Perhaps you could come over one Sunday?'

I agreed. I knew in my heart that what he was saying was right. Having read Matthew's Gospel I found it difficult to believe that Jesus would condone homosexual relationships. It just seemed so inconsistent with the rest of his moral teaching. Needless to say, I

A New Friend

was a bit reluctant to admit this change of attitude to Tim, because it seemed such an 'about-turn', remembering my efforts to persuade him to accept the homosexual lifestyle! Eventually, at a later meeting, I admitted to him that what Roy had said really did make sense. In my own thinking, the whole idea of loving other people in the way Jesus taught, including other men, gave me something positive and I thought potentially fulfilling. It seemed to be an exciting new way of possibly experiencing the love for which I knew I had always craved.

At this time I did not experience a strong desire to pick up someone for sex. My mind was too preoccupied with other things. However, there were still times when I would pass a familiar 'cruising spot' and almost stop the car from sheer force of habit. Each time this happened a voice within screamed, 'No!' Thoughts of losing all the ground I had gained, especially in my relationship with Tim, came flooding in and I was too fearful to give in to temptation.

A few weeks later Tim took me to Upton St Mary's, Roy Barker's church, and I was impressed by so much there. First, it was full. I had no idea that any churches attracted this many people! The general atmosphere was bright and friendly and the order of service was easy to follow, just a slip of paper in the back of the Psalter. Even I could not feel embarrassed. There was little formality in the service. You did not feel that a note or cough out of place, maybe a few words, would cause a stir to the congregation. It was even a surprise to hear Roy actually say, 'Good evening' at the start of the service and more of a surprise to hear the congregation reply. However, what impressed me more than anything else was the way in which the people there were talking together about what the Lord was doing in their lives. We could pick up little snippets of conversation as we waited in the long queue to leave the church building. I could identify with them and what they were saying, even as a newcomer to this relationship with Jesus. It made me feel at home more than anything else. There was a sense of being with like-minded people, even though I didn't know them. Strangely, I never stopped to think they may not understand my sexuality. I just felt at home.

Roy himself was a stockily built middle-aged man, with slightly thinning dark-brown hair. I was especially struck by his homely nature and gentle fatherly wisdom. His Yorkshire inflection and sense of humour were charming. 'I could probably relate to him, without feeling too daunted, or threatened' I thought.

Roy held a 'Vicar's Hour' on a Thursday evening, a bit like a doctor's surgery, and I decided to go through the Mersey Tunnel from Liverpool and see him. Thursday came and I made the 40-minute journey to Upton. On this first occasion I was a little late for the start of Vicar's Hour and a bit unsure of which door to use. I saw one or two people outside the vestry door of the church and guessed that must be the right one. I stayed in the car, trying to pluck up the courage to go in. Eventually it was too late – or at least I assumed it was because of the time. I returned home feeling defeated and depressed.

The next week I managed to see Roy and, like Tim, was struck by his warmth, friendliness and knowledge of 'the subject'. He seemed delighted at what had happened in my life and said, 'Who knows what the Lord has for you to do Martin? Perhaps even overseas missionary work!' He said it would always be nice to see me at St Mary's, but felt really a more local church would be better. He made a point of saying how important it was for me to become involved in the local church. He mentioned a few possibilities in the Liverpool area.

I was worried Roy might attempt to dissuade me from continuing the relationship with Tim, although I was prepared for this. However, he didn't, which encouraged me. Meanwhile I still continued to go to the gay pubs and clubs, as did Tim. A few of my friends knew something of what was happening in my life, although they were obviously suspicious that it was in order to please Tim, rather than anything else.

I tried various churches in Liverpool and became something of a 'spiritual gypsy' but nothing really compared with what I had experienced in Upton. I was very conscious of not appearing to be following Tim or putting too much pressure on him. I therefore sought to 'do my own thing', in terms of churchgoing, to establish my own Christian identity. There was always the thought in the back of my mind that I might be doing all this to keep Tim's friendship. Was my love for the Lord really more important to me than Tim?

Then, all of a sudden Tim's job moved him to London. In some ways I was sad about this; in other ways relieved. It meant the pressure of deciding to see him or not was no longer there, and I

A New Friend

would be able to continue my Christian experience without wondering about what he was thinking and how often I could see him. It would also help to prove my sincerity to my friends. My mother and father knew that I had started going to church and said they were pleased about this. At first they compared it with my brother's experience, but I think were soon convinced that it was very different. I also began to go to Upton far more frequently and saw Roy about the possibility of being confirmed in the Church of England. I was blissfully naïve and unaware of denominations at that stage. I still saw the Church as the traditional Church of England with a spire, bells and robes. Confirmation seemed necessary for me to affirm publicly that I had decided to follow Christ. Certainly my journey to that point of decision had been very unorthodox. All I could say was that God knew my vulnerable emotional needs and used them and of course Tim, to bring his love into my life.

Jesus told Nicodemus 'I tell you the truth, unless a man is born again, he cannot see the Kingdom of God' (John 3:3). I was beginning to appreciate the reality of that in my own life, as I found so many feelings and attitudes changing. I didn't fully understand the theological meaning of Jesus' words. It just seemed that God was at work in my life, before explaining to me what he was doing.

4

A Child in Christ

---◆◇◆---

As I read and understood more scripture, I found my new faith and experience made a lot of sense. A real thirst for God's word was there, despite the fact that for so many years reading books had not been one of my pastimes. My zeal to learn more helped me to concentrate, although my memory, especially for names, facts and figures, still leaves a lot to be desired! There were times when old insecurities re-surfaced, but I was aware of Jesus' presence in such a very real way that they were soon overcome. For example, I remember being with Tim in a club before he went to London and suddenly being overcome by a fear of losing my relationship with him. The next moment I felt Jesus put his arms around me and I knew comfort, assurance and peace. Nowadays it would probably be thought of as a type of 'prayer imagination'. I didn't work out the theological or spiritual implications at the time. I just knew Jesus was with me, so why should I not use my imagination to experience the reality of his presence?

As I became more involved at the church in Upton, so Christian fellowship became increasingly important to me. I wanted to share what God was doing in my life and hear more about him through others. There was a wonderful new freedom in not wanting to hide or pretend to be someone I was not. This also changed my attitude at work. They were a bit taken aback by the change in me. The swearing and the blaspheming had obviously stopped and I was getting used to the looks of amazement when I refused to 'rise to the bait' and respond in my old way to their jokes and comments. A few remarks like, 'We'll have to watch ourselves with holy Joe around!' were made, but on the whole there seemed to be a kind of acceptance. I had found a new ally in our manageress, who was a Christian. She was respected by nearly all the staff, although sometimes joked about. I now had more respect for her than ever before. She had been with us many years before I was born and, despite our being situated in a tough, 'red light' district of Liverpool, she still blushed if anyone swore or used obscene language, usually pretending not to hear. Sadly, in some ways, my Christianity made me feel a loss of identity with the other bakehouse workers, because our lifestyles were now even more different than before. At least I no longer felt I had to convince them I was a womaniser! Even though I didn't want my bakehouse friends to know about my homosexual past, my freedom from gay involvement made me feel I was no longer hiding anything. Witnessing was something my church fellowship encouraged and occasionally I overcame my reserve and shared my new-found faith with others. I nervously tuned the bakehouse radio into *Prayer for the Day*, *Thought for the Day* and *Pause for Thought* – sometimes even the Morning Service. The volume was gingerly raised, unless the talk was not Bible-based or evangelical, in which case I rapidly turned it down! I felt the Lord had carefully placed my workbench underneath the radio shelf for a specific purpose! There were a few complaints, but normally just a rather embarrassed silence. I was very conscious that they must see the 'change' in me and therefore refused to lose my temper. Nowadays I wonder how much of a real human being they saw in me and how effective my so-called witness really was!

Another sense of freedom I experienced was in finding myself in parts of Liverpool where in the past I would have looked for sexual contacts. Before, I would have worked out a series of excuses for being there, just in case the police or anyone I knew came by. Now, because I no longer had the same motivations and desires, my defences were not necessary. It felt good to be innocent. This also applied to my car, which had been renewed since I became a Christian. It is possible that the police knew of my other car, as I think the vice squad made a note of cars seen around notorious homosexual pick-up points, but I knew for certain that my new car would not be on their records.

The Lord had also given me a new desire to help other people. A way of fulfilling this need, it seemed, could be through working for a voluntary counselling organisation, so I joined the Samaritans. This is not a Christian organisation as such but was the only one I knew which took voluntary help. I should explain that there is a rule that no volunteer is to declare himself or herself; but I have not been involved with them for many years now. The preparation course was very helpful and interesting, although I was nervous at times and daunted by the prospect of trying to help people in perhaps a crisis situation. When I began work I made continual cries to the Lord for help and strength to cope, which he supplied.

I remember one occasion when I was the only male on duty in the centre when a very drunk and angry man was banging on the door and demanding to be let in. 'Arrow prayers' were going up thick and fast as I made my way towards him. It seemed quite likely from his mood that he would attack me – we could see him through the window even punching his own shadow! When I eventually opened the door and met him face to face I suddenly felt a tremendous love for him and to my amazement (as a 'number one coward') fear evaporated and the expression on his face transformed. I saw warmth, love and gentleness in his eyes. I was able to reason with him and help him on his way. Although we were not supposed to talk about our faith, the leaders knew my reason for joining was a Christian commitment, and I soon found God provided me with opportunities. Needless to say I quite often failed to make the most of them, although I was amazed how they were provided, without any need to break the rules. For example, a client would ask, 'I don't know if you're religious, but would you please pray for me!' Often I would be asked for my opinion by a client, and having explained the rules that we can only 'suggest' not 'advise', would be given permission to share my belief and faith. I obviously made it very clear that it was my own Christian belief, not the view or policy of the organisation. The commitment of the volunteers I met and their real love and concern for others made a lasting impression on me. Their motivation seemed to come from this love of others, rather than any Christian or religious ideology. The way it was, and I know is still expressed, continues to challenge me. Sadly, many of us who follow Christ often don't show this kind of unconditional love to others.

This work was to prepare me in many ways for the future, but one of the greatest things I gained from it was an understanding and love for my own brother. I heard about and met so many people with similar personality and psychological problems that I no longer saw evil in him, but instead the hurt and trauma of a complex personality problem. I still found it difficult to relate to him, but it was now in a completely different way. A love for him was there, even though feebly expressed.

At this time I was still seeing something of my old friends and occasionally had a meal with them. I was beginning to find these social evenings a bit difficult because of a strong internal conflict. I desperately wanted them to see the change God had brought to my life, so that they would seek him themselves. They would chat with me in the same way as in the past. However, I now not only had nothing to give to the conversation as far as sex, boyfriends and other interests were concerned, but often felt offended by their language and jokes. This really hurt me because I knew my language and crude, blasphemous sense of humour used to be far worse than theirs. I think they sensed my uneasiness, which caused some tension in the atmosphere. In some ways I was almost scared to be 'me' and felt I had to come over as a new and different person, a radiant and transformed Christian without any problems or difficulties. It was much later that God showed me how his love, and the way of Christ, is not as simple and painless as that. Many years afterwards, one of my former gay friends made a remark which meant a lot to me. He said, 'Dear Martin you haven't changed – you're still as dizzy as ever!' If he had said that during the early part of my Christian life, I would have reacted very differently and felt discouraged. I felt so conscious of the need to appear to be totally transformed, that a sense of the value in my basic humanity was not really appreciated. I wrongly felt I had to appear to be totally different in order to witness to the life-changing power of Christ.

Many of my gay friends were still staying overnight when they visited me, and they would sleep together. At first I thought nothing of this, but I began to question if it was honouring to the Lord for me to say that homosexual sex is wrong and then allow it to take place in my own house. It seemed I would have to say something to them – but how? I was horrified at what I thought their reaction might be. It could appear that I was rejecting them. They would have every right to tell me to get lost – to disown me. I phoned Dave, my closest friend and the one who seemed the most sympathetic to my Christian commitment. I began, 'Dave . . . I think there is something I need to say to you and the others but . . . Oh boy, it's so difficult – you've got every right to tell me to get lost . . .' Eventually, with a little help and encouragement from him, I was able to explain what I thought, and why. To my amazement he said, 'Martin, don't worry about it, I understand. There's no need to mention it again. If you like I can tell the others. It won't make any difference, don't worry. It's great to see you so happy, but I don't think it's for me.' I was overjoyed that the Lord had prepared his heart so wonderfully. I told the others myself and they were equally understanding. Their graciousness still amazes me, when they could have seen my remarks as a rejection and criticism of them personally.

In fact I was especially humbled by Ken's reaction. He moved back to London to be near his beloved Royal Opera House and set up home with a male partner. Ken wanted his new partner, John, to visit Liverpool and especially to meet me! He said, 'Martin, please don't be offended, but could you find us a hotel to stay in, because we know and respect your feelings? We don't want you to be hurt or embarrassed in any way.' I was horrified at the idea of Ken and John staying in a hotel, rather than with me, and told him so. He then said, 'Well perhaps we could sleep in separate rooms?' I was embarrassed and questioned if it was right for me to take such a firm stand. Ken sensed this, 'Don't say another word Martin. That's settled, we will stay with you and sleep in separate rooms.' They did and we had great fun together, showing John the wonders of Merseyside and the Lake District.

In his book *Knowing God*, James Packer shares how the Lord often encourages new Christians with 'little sweeties' of experience. Then may come the time when they must rely on faith alone to sustain them through difficult times. Well, I was still a 'babe' in Christ and the Lord was constantly making me aware of his love and presence. At that stage it must still have been necessary to have 'little sweeties'. I wouldn't have admitted it at the time, but difficulties and temptations may have encouraged me to doubt the validity of all that God was doing. My old lifestyle could have been very appealing, if being a Christian had turned out to be a major struggle. The 'sweeties' of encouraging experiences from God continued.

Working from an early morning start in the bakery often led to overtiredness. Frequently, when driving home late at night I was aware of falling asleep at the wheel. Thankfully, a jolt by the kerb would wake me enough to continue. However, one night I was travelling from Ormskirk to my home on the outskirts of Liverpool down winding, unlit roads. I was only too aware of falling asleep at the wheel and asked the Lord to help me. I know the sensible step is always to pull over for a snooze, but I didn't want to do this, probably because it would make me even later for bed at home, with even less time before I was up at 4.45 am. I am convinced that I fell asleep at the wheel that night. I cannot remember anything from drifting into sleep while driving down a country road, to waking up with a start and suddenly slamming on my brakes – in my drive, at home! I had motored down a lane, turned into the large open-plan housing estate, with identical houses and driven onto my own driveway, while still unconscious! My first reaction when I woke up was that the Lord had driven me home and I thanked him. When I told my non-Christian friends they were not impressed . . . 'You can do things automatically.' I replied, 'Sure, but not if your eyes are closed!' It was several years later that I heard about angels. Psalm 91:11 says, 'For he will command his angels concerning you to guard you in all your ways; they will lift you up in their hands, so that you will not strike your foot against a stone.' This made a lot of sense to me and I realised that angels had protected me then and on several occasions before and since. Those who know my driving will certainly testify to this.

As I read more of God's word, the Lord not only seemed to speak to my everyday situation, but also showed me how much his pattern for our lives made sense. As I learned more, I longed to share it with others, especially Tim, now in London. Sadly he often felt threatened by this and sometimes thought I was 'getting at him'. I was too insensitive and clumsy to realise this. In fact I know now that he was right – I *was* trying to 'get at him'! I worried that he was apparently not getting as involved in a Christian lifestyle as I was and could always see the possibility of his deeper involvement in the gay lifestyle. London was certainly a likely place for this to happen. Tim was very attractive, both in looks and personality, and often seemed to get into difficult situations. Someone would make it clear they were attracted to him and smile or glance his way. He would sometimes feel honour-bound to respond, which often caused problems and sometimes resulted in a sexual encounter. We already had a small circle of gay friends in London, but Tim had no regular church commitment.

Meanwhile the only Christian fellowship I had was through my visits to Upton, for church meetings and Sunday services. The regular confirmation classes were a great encouragement for me, as we talked and shared our faith together under Roy Barker's leadership. He explained so many ways of applying one's faith and shared a lot of his personal testimony. Roy also did everything possible to make sure that Christians were exercising a ministry. His phone calls – '. . . I've got a little job I thought you might like to do . . .' – were notorious. It is so important that Christians are able to feel they are doing something for the Lord and within his Kingdom. I believe God created that need within us, both for our own sense of value and for each other. Roy encouraged me to go out with one of his lay ministers, who used to visit and have some pastoral responsibility for areas of the parish. This certainly helped me to overcome some of my shyness and encouraged me to share my faith. It was also very interesting to sit in on the lay ministers' meetings, as they shared about their own experiences of visiting. Why was I chosen to be involved in this, when I had only been a Christian for a relatively short time (not much more than a year) and was so shy? There is no doubt that Roy's God-given wisdom had seen this as the best way forward for me and, as usual, Roy had thrown convention to the wind.

My confirmation was a wonderful event for me, with my father, mother and brother all attending, plus some Christian aunts, uncles and cousins – the ones I used to keep at arm's length and find a bit strange, but now could identify with in a new way. Tim did say he would try to make my confirmation, but could not promise. Before the service there was no sign of him and I assumed he was not there. Then, as I stood up and turned around after the Bishop laid hands on me, the first person I saw in the congregation was Tim. Our eyes met and we smiled. I thought it was a wonderful touch of God's love.

Now that the commitment of the confirmation classes was over, my midweek visits to Upton were a little less frequent. I had not made any really close friends over there, but at that stage did not seem too concerned. I was still discovering so much that was exciting in my relationship with Jesus, everything else seemed less important. I even gave away my two Burmese cats, to whom I was devoted. 'I don't need them now', I figured, 'I've got the Lord Jesus.'

Then, after one Sunday evening service at St Mary's, I had an experience that seemed so strange that for years I hesitated to share it. At the end of the service I noticed a whole row of figure eights at the top of the hymn text we had just sung. Then I glanced at the notice-board, which said 'Eighth after Trinity'. I had never attached any importance to numbers before. On the way home I found myself compulsively noting numbers on road signs or car licence plates. The number eight kept reappearing. Even if I added numbers together it always made eight. In no way do I have a mathematical brain, but every time I added two of the numbers I saw together, it came to eight! For example, the motorway home was the M53 (5 + 3 = 8). I then started to think of dates and add them together. The same thing happened, yet as I said before, my brain does not function well enough to know beforehand the end product of any numbers I add. 'The date of my confirmation was 26 September (2 + 6 = 8). My birthday is the 14 March (third month – 1 + 4 + 3 = 8). And so it went on . . . ! I kept telling myself, 'Stop . . . this is ridiculous!'

When I arrived home I opened the Bible Tim had given me and noticed the text in the front. It read, 'Jesus said, "If you continue in my word, you are truly my disciples, and you will know the truth, and the truth will make you free"' (John 8:31, 32).

'Funny, "eight" again!' I thought. I felt a bit stupid and really doubted that it meant anything. 'Was I going slightly mad?' I wrote a brief letter to Tim and noticed his address . . . '80' . . . 'This has got to stop!'

The next morning at 4.45 I was in my usual semi-conscious state, about to put the kettle on for a morning 'fix' of coffee to waken me, when I noticed a Red Admiral butterfly flapping helplessly around the small kitchen. 'How odd', I thought. First, butterflies had been very scarce that year, and second, I had never known one to be trapped indoors like that. Moths yes, frequently, but never butterflies. In my still somewhat dozy state I carefully manoeuvred it towards the window, which I opened to release it into the fresh air. As it made for freedom the Lord said, 'You've set it free. You will be setting others free.' I was stunned. There are times when you wonder if that inner voice is really the Lord. Sometimes, the words are so meaningful and detached from any conscious thought or idea that you had. Then you can feel more convinced that the voice is not simply your imagination. This was such an occasion. For the rest of that day I was still in a fairly dazed state. By the next day I had recovered. I figured it was another of 'those experiences'! That Wednesday I decided to go to the midweek church meeting. I had not been for several weeks. The person leading the Bible study started to speak, 'Tonight we are going to look at John Chapter Eight!' I was stunned, yet again. As I looked around the open Bibles before me, the pages almost seemed to be glowing with a brilliant white, like the washing powder adverts. I really must have been very moved because I stood up and shared, without going into every detail (I was too embarrassed), what I felt the Lord had been saying. I was still puzzled, not really knowing what it all meant. Many years later, it became clear.

The family business was due to be closed down because of a compulsory purchase order. I had no great interest in the business and thought, with my Samaritan experience behind me, that I would like to do some sort of social work. However, it was all a bit uncertain. It seemed logical for me to think about moving to Upton because there was only a small mortgage on my house in Liverpool and a cheaper one could be bought in Upton to clear it. I was very fond of my Liverpool home, but the advantages of being within easy walking distance of the church, rather than 40 minutes away by car, clinched it. I moved, and my parents bought my house to use for their retirement. It all worked out very well indeed. For a while, until we finally closed the bakery, I commuted to work from Upton. We had a farewell party in my house and I will never forget the ordeal of simply sharing a few words with the staff before we made some presentations. It gives an indication of just how shy I was to say that – even with people I knew in my own home, speaking out loud and hearing my own voice was very traumatic – the sweat poured off me.

Once settled into my new home it was really good to be nearer church. However, it was not quite as I had imagined. People did not just pop in, unless invited. I still felt quite lonely and most of my friends were married. I began to get more involved with a group of mainly single people. A curate from the church, John, was always very warm and loving to me and we were beginning to get to know one another. He was tall and slim with immaculately groomed long black hair and beard. Many people remarked that he looked like Jesus – that is, the Hollywood version!

Before the bakery finally closed and I was on the dole, I decided to have a little party to which I would invite my closest homosexual friends and some of the Christians I knew at church. The motive behind this was to witness to my friends and help them to see what had been happening in my life. The Christians were from many different social, academic and even denominational backgrounds. Most of them had led a fairly 'sheltered' life, but were apparently

A Child in Christ

almost unshockable. Having originally told them that I was inviting some of my non-Christian friends, it suddenly dawned on me that though they all knew about my own homosexual background, they may not realise that all these friends would also be homosexual. I hastily phoned round and said, 'I think you ought to know . . . well, all of my friends coming are homosexual!' A typical response was, 'Fine Martin . . . what time did you say you wanted us to arrive?' As far as my gay friends were concerned, I am sure they felt it was a bit like 'throwing the pagans into the Christian Lion's Den'. John had a good chat with one man from Manchester and came into the kitchen, obviously greatly encouraged. 'Martin, he asked if we could go and spend the weekend with him. Is that OK with you?' I agreed, then about half an hour later a somewhat crestfallen John said to me, 'I think we'd better call off the weekend. I think he's got the wrong idea! I so much want to tell him I love him but I'm scared that it might be misinterpreted!' It seemed he had been gently propositioned! At one stage a Christian woman went up to another friend of mine, gazed into his handsome face and said, 'You're not like the others, are you? You're not homosexual?' There was a very embarrassed reply, 'Well . . . er . . . Yes I am!'

'But you can't be!' she gasped, 'I know girls who would queue from here down the street for a date with you!'

One of my friends did get slightly drunk and I was concerned that a strictly teetotal, non-smoking, no television, elderly Christian lady and prayer warrior would have been offended. When asked, she replied, 'Oh no Martin, I believe the Lord used the alcohol to loosen his tongue!'

It was certainly an unusual evening, but I doubted its success in quite the way I'd envisaged it.

Before long, Roy Barker organised a 'consultation at the vicarage' for anyone wishing to meet up with someone whom Christ had brought out of homosexuality. It was mentioned in the church magazine and it was not long before the local 'gay group' heard about it. They contacted him to ask if they could send some representatives. Roy thought it was a great idea. They were 'nibbling at his bait'. It was a very intimate meeting with the two gay men, myself and four Christians from my church. I knew the men from the gay group quite well and they were really taken aback to see me there. In my enthusiasm I talked about 'victory', 'bondage' and used other evangelical terminology which had become so much a part of my vocabulary. As might be expected, they took offence at the use of these words and were verbally aggressive and abusive. It seemed they were under the impression they had been invited to talk to *us* about homosexuality! Roy graciously pointed out this was not quite the way it had been intended. Eventually they stopped protesting and one of them said, 'Maybe we ought to know more about this Jesus you are all talking about!' Roy moved in quickly . . . 'But you can . . .' and so they did.

One evening I gave my testimony at an after-church meeting in my home. I had decided, after talking it through with one or two others, that I should be perfectly open about my way of life and not be concerned about shocking them too much. So I was perfectly open, and afterwards it seemed as if I had been talking about a Sunday School outing – there was no obvious shock expressed at all. Any event like this usually filled me with horror because of my shyness, becoming a mighty event on my calendar, which I worried about for days or weeks ahead. On this occasion I was quite at ease.

Soon we were using my house for the young people's meetings. We called it 'Senior CYFA' and some of us were a lot more 'senior' than others! My relationship with John and the other curate, Mark, developed and we became friends, although there were the sort of limits on the relationships one would expect at this stage, with a curate and parishioner. I still felt something of a loner and wondered if there could really be anyone else like me from a homosexual background. I also became very conscious of the way in which churches divide people into groupings: 'Marrieds', 'Singles', 'Old Wives', 'Young Wives', 'Youth Groups', 'Pensioners', and so on. I found it difficult to understand and appreciate because among my homosexual friends those barriers were not so apparent. I understood the special situations and experiences that each of those groups needed to share with one another, but I found it difficult to see why they were all really necessary.

5
Love Often Hurts

After a couple of weeks on the dole, the bakery having closed in 1974, Roy Barker offered me a job as the Church Hallkeeper. This was caretaking work, opening and closing the hall for various organisations and keeping it clean. It meant I had to be on call many times during the day and evening, but with lots of spare time. Roy, John and I wondered if the Lord could be calling me into the ordained ministry, and this was a good time to explore that idea.

My relationship with John was deepening, but in keeping with my other relationships it was rather superficial. This was probably because with both men and women I always tended to wait for the other person to make the first move of friendship towards me. There was always a nagging doubt that they would reject me. There may have been an element of fear on their part, because of my background and, perhaps, their inability to identify with my past and present situation. It was many years before I learned to recognise this fear in many of my friends.

The Bible says, 'We love God because he first loved us' (1 John 4:19). My love for God and dependence on him were now increasing as he revealed more and more of his love to me. Also John's warm, loving and sensitive nature really attracted me. He seemed a vulnerable person, but with a strong, striking personality, and his loving concern and charisma attracted a lot of people to him. I found a deep love developing, but did not feel shame about it. I shared my feelings with him, telling him there was nothing required in return, and found I could love in an exciting new way, in accordance with Scripture. For a while John's relationship with me was not much deeper than that which he shared with many others in our Senior CYFA group. To my amazement I felt quite content with this, provided I was allowed to love, and I made an effort not to put any pressure on him.

Then one weekend we were all away at a houseparty and it became pretty clear that John was very depressed. He shared the great burden on his heart, which involved a difficult relationship with a girl in the parish. It has been said that one of the greatest gifts of love is self-disclosure. If we are prepared to share something with someone, we are saying, 'I am trusting you.' John's gift of love to me meant a lot, and I was apparently one of the very few people who knew his secret. He eventually said that it was going to be very difficult for him to prepare his sermon. For John, preparation usually meant many hours of sweat and toil, with copious notes, but on this occasion he could not get down to it. Then, again taking me into his confidence, he said that he felt he should share his testimony when he spoke.

It was one of the most moving sermons I have ever heard. Many times John almost broke down in the pulpit as he shared his life with us. Then he told us in a tremendously humble way how much being a popular charismatic leader had done for his ego. 'If you follow me you'll be in a mess', he said, 'because I'm in a mess – but if you follow Jesus his strength will be made perfect through weakness.' His text was 'We have this treasure in earthen vessels' (2 Cor. 4:7).

At the end, Roy stood up and thanked John for all he had shared. He added, 'If he thinks he is weak, then I am ten times weaker.' John had requested as a final hymn 'Peace, perfect peace, in this dark world of sin', but very few of us could sing, we were so chocked with emotion. I was, as usual, not able to express my emotions during the service, but afterwards, as I listened to the recording, I wept. I shared in the pain he was expressing, as my relationship with John and his girlfriend meant so much to me. The two of them often invited me to join them at the cinema, or they simply popped in for a quiet evening. If I ever made noises about being a 'gooseberry', I was just told to be quiet. John frequently called in late at night, when we would sit and natter, or just relax with music, for hours. Then at perhaps 2am we would decide to make some porridge! It was crazy, but wonderful.

I often felt depressed and condemned when my shyness prevented me praying out loud at meetings. John used to give me a very 'knowing' and loving look and silently mouth, 'Are you all right?' I often felt embarrassed on these occasions, wondering what on earth people would be thinking. Would they think *he* was homosexual? However, it meant so much to know that he was prepared to show his love without concern for what others might think. He was prepared to be seen as a friend of mine. Does that not remind you of Jesus' love – 'the friend of tax collectors and sinners'? It was a new experience for me to be loving two people as much as Tim and John, without feeling threatened or insecure. Jealousy and possessiveness did not seem to be a problem. Without feeling like some kind of masochistic martyr, I felt I could give in a way which brought positive purpose to these relationships. David Watson once said, 'Love that cost nothing is worth what it costs – nothing.' However, I tended not to move towards other people in our group and relate on such a deep level with them as I did with John. I wanted to protect John and his girlfriend's privacy, the fact they felt it necessary to keep their relationship secret. I doubt that this prevented any other possible relationships developing for me. If it did, it was a cost very gladly borne, as I learnt more from John at this time than from any other person.

When someone you love very much is hurting, then of course you are hurting with them. Often there is a sense of real helplessness when you feel there is nothing you can do, because it might put too much pressure on the person concerned. With John and Tim it seemed that their crises rarely coincided, but once they did. I remember crying helplessly to God, 'Oh Lord, why do I love them so much?' Immediately came the reply, 'Because I do.' It was an instant response to my question: it must be from the Lord. I could never have thought of anything as profound yet simple, so quickly! As I thought about these words, they encouraged me yet again to continue on this road of costly loving. I have needed to learn the lesson over and over again. I was beginning to know something of the qualities of love in 1 Corinthians 13, but there was (and is) a long way to go down that path. In many ways I was far too arrogant in thinking I was pretty good at selfless loving! I was not aware enough of the pressure it can put on the one you love, when you say you don't want anything in return. I guess very few, if any, of us are able to receive 'unconditional love' without wondering how we should respond and maybe questioning motives. I wonder how many of my attempts to love unconditionally are really as unconditional as I try to convince myself?

I was able to meet Tim's family. That is, those who were Christians: his sister, brother-in-law, and sisters-in-law. He was very much on edge in case they found out about his homosexuality, although deep down he still thought his sister and her husband, Jane and Andrew, ought to know. I spent a few days with the family in the Lake District. It was a wonderful new experience for me. We walked through the beautiful scenery and would sometimes just stop and thank the Lord for the marvel of his creation. With all these new influences I began to see how much I had missed in my late teens and early twenties. Life had been so sex-orientated that other hobbies, interests and sports were ignored. Tim and his family had been into horse riding and various other activities. I envied them and really felt I had missed out. Music was also something Christians seemed to be quite good at. Many played the guitar and piano. Was it too late for me to start, at 30?

I had little experience in relating to women as friends. My schooldays were very much an all-male environment. My gay friends had all been male. I felt more comfortable with men, simply because it was familiar territory for me. I was now getting to know many women as friends and feeling much more comfortable in their presence. I guess it was a lot to do with our common experience of Christ. We shared a sense of identity as Christians, but I was also beginning to understand and identify with women emotionally. I now realise that many men with homosexual feelings relate well to women, even though there may be no strong emotional and sexual attraction. But for me this was a new experience. I still found it difficult to identify with Tim's desire to settle down and have a family. There were quite a few women at church with whom I really felt at home and I enjoyed being with them, but could not envisage marriage in any way. In St Mary's it was becoming increasingly clear how much emotional trauma so many single Christian women face. I found it gave me a great feeling of empathy with them, but made me a bit wary, just in case any had ideas of me as a potential marriage partner! Thankfully, this was very rare indeed. Either the women were not interested in me, or just felt I was a 'hopeless case'.

It was a great joy to use my home for hospitality to visiting speakers and sometimes Christian musicians, dancers and actors. I guess the latter revitalised my old interests in theatre. I was greatly blessed to meet some of the Swedish choir, 'Choralerna', and to get to know them. When I knew they were also visiting London I wanted Tim to meet them, as I believed the Lord was directing me to lead Tim into a church fellowship. He still had not settled in one and, although he always intended to do something about it, never did! In my usual approach, as sensitive as a 'sledge-hammer', I determined to go down to London for the weekend, to impress Tim with 'Choralerna' and find him a church. I made enquiries and a suitable church was found.

In the meantime Tim had become very friendly with a dancer called Michael, who was homosexual. Tim had told him about God and said he wondered if the Lord would move in Michael's life as he had in mine. I met Michael that weekend and it soon became obvious that he was very much in love with Tim. Many feelings and emotions were whirling inside me, as it seemed like a dangerous situation. Jealously was one of them, although I was reluctant to admit it to myself. Michael was a very attractive person, but had not responded to the Gospel at all. I felt he was living in hope of having a homosexual relationship with Tim, and that frightened me. Where could the relationship go from here? It could only hurt Michael or possibly drag Tim into a homosexual relationship, from which he might not have the will, power or desire to escape. Where was the Lord in all this? I believed I had to persuade Tim to break off the relationship, but was aware that he would think it was more of a jealous tantrum on my part, than the Lord.

After a lot of soul-searching and heartache prayer, I felt I knew what I had to say to him, but dreaded the idea of a confrontation. I shared, as honestly as I could, what I was feeling. Then I said in order to prove to myself and to him that my motives were right, that I was prepared to end our own relationship, once he had finished with Michael and settled in a church fellowship. It did not seem right for me to let go completely, until I knew he was in a fellowship. Tim seemed a bit reluctant, feeling that Michael might still come to the Lord. I was a bit scared that he would take me at my word and end our relationship. He agreed to come with me to the local church I had found. During the last hymn, Tim suddenly broke down. I was stunned and felt helpless; I longed to put my arms around him and comfort him, but felt too shy, though I made a feeble attempt at it. He eventually composed himself and left, having chatted briefly to the vicar, who had obviously seen his distress and wanted to help. Once in the car, he broke down again and sobbed, realising that I was right and he must end the relationship with Michael. Then it was my turn to start sobbing uncontrollably – an unusual experience for me. I had no idea he had felt quite so strongly about Michael and it now seemed that I had been responsible for hurting Tim. I not only felt his hurt, but thought I caused it. We ended up comforting one another. Tim said, 'You know I really didn't want you to come down this weekend, but now I don't want you to go!'

Later that evening, when I arrived home, Tim phoned. 'Something amazing has happened', he said. 'I called in to see Jane and Andrew, and Jane said, 'What's the matter Tim?' and I broke down. She said, 'Is it a girl? . . . Is it a man?' Martin, I have been able to share everything with her and Andrew. They were marvellous!' I was really able to share in his joy. He said he would see Michael the next day and explain everything. We both prayed and agreed that the Lord would prepare that situation as he had done everything else. He did. Michael agreed with Tim that it was hopeless to continue together and Tim said, although it was very difficult and painful, that he felt a sense of relief in 'giving Michael to God'.

As far as my possible ordination was concerned, a selection conference was arranged and I went in great fear and trembling. It was thrilling to see the Lord overrule and give me so much strength and confidence. I was certain I must have been accepted, but they turned me down on the grounds I may not be able to cope with the academic work required in training. It really hurt: was God playing games with me – to give me the confidence and assurance, only to take it away? I felt hurt, only this time by God.

Roy Barker was a marvellous encouragement, of course, and having consulted with the Director of Ordinands, felt it right that I should take some 'O' level exams to prove that I could cope with the academic work necessary to train for the ministry. Eventually, it was felt I should probably apply again and I continued working at the Church Hall, while getting two 'O' levels.

One night at eleven, I had a phone call from the hospital to say that my mother, who had a heart condition, had been admitted and was in intensive care. I phoned John to ask him to pray. Despite being thoroughly exhausted (I had only just driven him home, because he was too tired to drive) he insisted on coming over to the hospital in Liverpool with me. This obviously meant a lot to me and my father. I remember wanting to pray with my mother as she lay unconscious in intensive care, surrounded by medics and equipment. I remembered seeing a hospital chaplain I knew praying with someone in a coma. He was unconscious, but when my friend asked him to put his hand into the hand of Jesus, I was amazed to see it move very slightly. I was too self-conscious and one of the people attending mother gently motioned for us to leave. A few minutes later we were told that my mother had just died. She was 69. I could see God's hand in the situation very clearly. My father's best friend was on one of his rare visits at the time and John was there for me. God proved to be Lord of life and death as well as comforter. John took the funeral, which was a wonderful witness to God's goodness and faithfulness. I was still unable to cry. The responsibility for organising the funeral and sharing the news with relatives and friends was mine. I felt God's enabling so much at this time, but in some ways there was a sense of unreality about it. At least I no longer found funerals quite as scary and unfamiliar as in the past, because I was now helping with them at church.

On the whole I felt pretty good about all that God had been doing in my life, but I had real difficulty identifying or even sympathising with Christians struggling with problems I felt I no longer had. My thinking was that if God can do it for me then he will do it for everyone else. In terms of struggling with temptation and sins, my Christian life seemed to have been pretty smooth sailing. There had been an awareness of my own sinfulness in some areas and of emotional struggles, but there always seemed to be some kind of resolution to them. Sexual temptations had not really been an issue. I regarded this as pretty amazing considering how much my life had revolved around sex since my teenage years. My new way of life as a Christian was so very different from the past that sex didn't seem to be an issue any more. I hadn't masturbated for a couple of years. There were some times of sexual arousal, but the temptation to do anything about it was not really there. I imagined, without realising it, that God deals with us all in exactly the same way, as if there was some kind of spiritual formula that everyone should experience. I found it difficult to understand why struggling with sexual feelings and desires should really be a problem for committed Christians. Then one day I masturbated! It seemed to happen without a fantasy or desire. It shook me; after a few years as a Christian, how could this happen to me? I shared my feelings with John, who was probably surprised that I should make such an issue of it. My emotions had been rocked a bit. My homosexuality, at least the obviously sexual part of it, had resurfaced. Now I found I could

Still Learning to Love

identify with many of the people I had possibly even hurt by my lack of real understanding. The words of the Apostle Paul about his 'thorn in the flesh' (2 Cor. 12:7) had a whole new meaning for me. I really had been 'elated' in my new-found relationship with Jesus, but judgemental in my attitude to the problems other Christians face. I wouldn't have verbalised it, but Christianity seemed very straightforward to me. I thought you became a Christian and the Holy Spirit enabled you to overcome life's problems and difficulties. The 'honeymoon' period was over for me. I clearly had a lot more to learn about myself, others and, most importantly, God's ways.

Then John moved to Liverpool. The late-night porridge and chats had gone, and I began to feel lonely and sometimes even unloved. These were lies from Satan, maybe, but the 'little sweeties' from the Lord were also being replaced by more solid food. I was starting to appreciate something new about the 'treasure' Paul talks about in my 'jar of clay' (2 Cor. 4:7).

6
Vision of a Ministry

I PAID A VISIT TO THE EVANGELICAL SISTERS OF MARY at Canaan in Darmstadt, Germany. John had been there and came back thoroughly enthused. This community had been started just after the Second World War by two German women (Basilea and Mart). They were discovering the depth of love for the Lord Jesus that comes through repentance, leading to an understanding of the Cross and God's redemption. These women started a sisterhood based on sharing the truth of this joy and repentance with others. They believed they were called to a complete surrendering to Jesus Christ and a total dependence on God. Their definition of 'living by faith' doesn't mean asking other Christians for money, directly or indirectly, but literally keeping silent about finance and waiting for God to provide. Mother Basilea believed God had provided a place where others could find this 'first love for Jesus'. It was to be called 'The Land of Canaan' and built in Darmstadt, even though there were local authority plans for roads etc. on it. The women only had a few German Marks between them. The story of how this amazing and beautiful place was built really is a modern-day series of miracles of 'biblical proportions'. My time there showed me a new dimension of God's love, even though I only spent ten days with the Sisters and Canaan Brothers. Their humility and total surrender to God's will in their lives is something I shall always remember and admire.

The time at Canaan with the Sisters of Mary had not only helped to establish within me a deeper understanding of the cost to Jesus of my redemption, but also the need to bring to him all my sins, not just the obvious ones. The sisters encouraged us to see the many sins in our lives, in order that we will know even more of Jesus' love and forgiveness. In other words, the more sinful we know we are, the more we should know the extent of God's love. For example, I thought I was pretty humble and aware of my inadequacies. But at

Canaan I realised how judgemental I could be. Sometimes, in subtle ways, I had seen the 'speck' in my brother's or sister's eye, when there was a great big plank in my own! Sins were uncovered that I had not realised were there. For example, the Lord showed me that I was conceited. 'How can I be?' I thought, 'when I am so shy and often aware of my weaknesses?' Mother Basilea pointed out that if we keep examining our actions in the mirror of our minds and continually wonder what others are thinking of us, then we are proud and conceited. It is a form of self-idolatry – that was me all right!

I wish I could say I continued to live in the way modelled for me during my time in Germany. But having returned from this heavy 'spiritual injection' in my life, my lifestyle soon slipped into a fairly mundane pattern again. Working at the Church Hall and studying for my 'O' levels filled nearly all my time. My father travelled over on my day off and spent nearly all the day with me. My relationships with most people were fairly superficial, compared to what I had experienced with Tim and John. They were still a part of my life, but not a lot was happening between us. We were certainly not as involved with one another as we had been. In the neighbourhood and church I had become very much a part of the environment. I was no longer the new Christian, whom the Lord had dramatically changed. I was now part of the 'establishment' at home, virtually all my social contact being with other Christians. My gay friends kept in touch, usually through Christmas cards. We always said it would be nice to meet up again but, without verbalising we probably agreed we no longer had much in common.

It was time to take stock. What had the Lord done in my life? Where should I go from here? It seemed probable that I would go forward again for ordination, eventually. I was still operating as a lay minister in the church, but usually needed a hefty kick before I would actually go out visiting. On every occasion I actually pushed myself out and started 'door knocking', the Lord blessed and uplifted me, considerably. Again and again I had seen how easy it is for Satan to convince me that I had nothing to give. Apathy set in, together with a type of spiritual depression. Once that is broken through and the lies of the enemy are exposed, the Lord moves and blessings are received.

In July 1976 Gerald Coates wrote a very honest and well-balanced article about homosexuality in *Crusade* magazine which meant a lot to me, because here was a Christian who had been prepared to share something of his homosexual past. I had still not talked with another Christian from a homosexual background. I felt I must write to *Crusade* and thank them, sharing a bit of my own experience, and wondered if I should use my address. Considering what I shared in the letter, it seemed very hypocritical not to do so, but I felt rather exposed. As usual, I hesitated before taking any action. When the letter was finally sent it was too late for the edition carrying readers' reactions to Gerald's article. However, I noticed to my great relief that under every letter printed were the words, 'Name and address supplied'. 'Praise the Lord!' I thought, 'They won't print my name and address, after all!' A month later I received the next copy of *Crusade* from our church distributor as I was leaving the Sunday morning service. I was outside the church with a couple of friends who knew me quite well and about 300 other churchgoers. I opened my *Crusade* and rapidly turned to the 'Letters' section. My eyes suddenly spotted the words, 'Martin Hallett, Upton, Wirral'. I screamed in horror. One of my friends turned towards me and I showed her the page. She laughed and said, 'Now you really have nailed your colours to the mast! Praise the Lord!' My stomach was still turning over with embarrassment. It was a strange feeling, almost like being in a public place and suddenly realising that I had no clothes on (which happens to be a recurring nightmare of mine!).

I felt terribly self-conscious for several weeks. It made me realise that after my initial desire to be open with everyone when I first became a Christian, there were many people I knew in church who had had no idea of my background. One such person, a missionary home on furlough, came up to me after church one Sunday. She gently squeezed my arm and whispered in my ear, 'I saw your letter in *Crusade*. Praise the Lord – it's wonderful.' There were one or two other quiet words of encouragement, which helped me to overcome my fears.

The repercussions from that letter were remarkable. Roy Barker had a phone call from someone called Geoffrey Percival saying that he believed the person who wrote a letter in *Crusade* went to Roy's church. Geoffrey would be very interested to meet Martin Hallett because of a ministry that he and one or two people from the Nationwide Festival of Light were about to launch.

Eddy and Irene Stride (Rector of Christchurch, Spitalfields, London, and his wife) have a wonderful gift of hospitality. Geoffrey

Percival and Bob Hill were staying together at the Strides, where the topic of my letter in *Crusade* was mentioned. Geoff was on his way to Poole in Dorset to launch a new ministry to homosexuals, to be called Pilot. Bob had been a member of my church, St Mary's, in the past and still had many friends there, and he certainly knew of me. Except for this 'God-incidence' of a meeting it is unlikely that I would have met Geoff. I could have found out about Pilot in the course of time, but may not have contacted him, except possibly for help – if my pride allowed it!

Some friends of mine in Upton offered me a holiday in Bournemouth, staying in their mother's house. This seemed an ideal opportunity to meet Geoff. He was easy to relax with and reminded me a bit of my slightly eccentric friend, Richard, although Geoff had no 'upper-crust accent' and certainly not Richard's homosexual inclinations! Many years of experience with Eric Hutching's evangelistic team had left Geoff with much to share and give, and with the ability to communicate the personal application of basic biblical principles clearly and often amusingly.

I was intrigued by the way he had converted the church vestry, from which he operated, into a 'home from home'. There was a nice green Wilton carpet covering the floor, a couple of smart chairs, desk and filing cabinet; also some cooking facilities and a portable television in the corner. It seemed more like a smart study or small living room than a church vestry. It was Geoff's little world. When not answering the phone, writing or seeing people, he would perhaps help to tidy the church graveyard outside or walk down to the harbour and town of Poole itself.

As Geoff and I talked, I became aware for the first time that there were some people professing to be born-again Christians, who believed that a homosexual relationship was compatible with Christianity. It really shocked me to read a letter written to Geoff by one of these people. It was not abusive in any way and talked about a personal relationship with Christ, in fact using all the evangelical language that I had come to identify with committed Christians who love the Lord Jesus. 'How could this person possibly believe God was pleased with and blessed his homosexual partnership?' I thought. It seemed to be so clear from the scriptures that it was wrong. I had read books by David Field and Roger Moss which had served to underline my own thoughts on the subject. The early conviction that homosexual behaviour, but not orientation or temptation, was wrong had never been challenged. I had not really thought it through for myself yet. It just seemed that the texts by St Paul and the attitude of Jesus in themselves were enough for me. Now that I was firmly established in a Christian lifestyle, which upheld my beliefs, I really did not want to change my point of view. So the experience and beliefs of the person who wrote the letter left me puzzled and a bit angry, but at the same time challenged. It was reassuring to know that Geoff agreed with me.

I remembered my early Christian experience and realised how important the acceptance and understanding of other Christians had been to me. Certainly my relationships with Tim and John had brought a lot of love and fulfilment to my life. 'Was this not what all homosexuals are really searching for?' I thought. One evening, Geoff had an appointment to counsel a Christian man about his homosexual problems. He asked me if I would like to join them, and I agreed. I found myself becoming more and more fascinated by the prospect of actually meeting another Christian with homosexual feelings. It had always seemed as if there was just Tim and I who felt like this, although of course I knew there must be others. What would this man be like? Would he be attractive to me?

I was shocked at my reactions. There were hints of responses that I knew from my past. Was it more than just an old reflex action, or something much more serious? Whatever it was, I knew it must be 'crucified with Christ'. The curiosity itself still lingered, until I actually met this man, but I knew there was no question of any relationship, sexual or not. I stopped analysing my feelings so much and decided that I would enter this situation, no matter what my motives and responses might be. When I eventually joined Geoff and his contact, all I could think of was trying to help him.

My brief time with Geoffrey Percival in Poole had not only made me aware of the need for this type of ministry, but it gave me a burning desire to help in some way. As I mulled everything over in my mind and thought of my own experiences, some basic needs emerged that I felt were very important. It seemed to me that it was no good simply counselling people if there was not a church fellowship in which they would be loved, accepted and could grow in Christ. With all my complaints about being lonely, I remembered very clearly how non-judgemental and accepting Christians had been and still were to me. From what Geoff had shared about the fears and reluctance of many churches and individual Christians to face up to the homosexual issue, there seemed a very urgent need for positive teaching. If this did not happen, how many other Christians would join the ranks of the homosexual Christian who wrote to Geoff? Therefore, I thought the ideal type of ministry would be twofold: partly teaching the Church and partly pastoral support and counselling. I put these ideas down on paper, rather like a job description. I realised that I had created an idea for a workable ministry and wanted to give it some sort of title. The event of three years previously, when I released the trapped butterfly, came into mind. Since that time I had seen so many ways in which the 'truth had set me free'.

- Truth in terms of God's love.
- Truth about myself in weakness and strength.
- Truth in terms of honesty and openness with others. No more need to deceive or be a hypocrite.

All these and more had set me free in lots of ways, even though of course there was still a long way to go. Therefore the name must encompass somehow truth and freedom. I decided to call my idea 'True Freedom' and believed that God had given me this vision. When I thought of my little bit of counselling experience, the lay ministry and of course what I had been through in terms of my own homosexuality, it seemed the Lord had been preparing me for all this. Jesus said, 'Which of you, if his son asks for bread, will give him a stone?' (Matthew 7:9). The 'stone' that I thought had been my lot, when I was turned down for the ordained ministry, had really been 'bread'. It had been pointing to another door, which was just beginning to open.

Geoff shared with me the way the Lord had led him to set up Pilot. It had originally been planned to open a care centre, sponsored by the Nationwide Festival of Light and run by Geoff and a retired Salvation Army worker, Edward Shackleton. The people living at the centre would be homosexuals and other 'casualties of the permissive society', as they put it. But a lack of sufficient funds seemed to indicate that another direction and ministry was needed, and Pilot was born. Advertisements were placed in newspapers and a phone number given. Therefore, the majority of people contacting Pilot were not Christians. Mr Shackleton had a lifelong burden for this type of ministry. I hope and pray he was encouraged by all

God had done, when he went to be with the Lord several years later in 1985.

I shared my vision of True Freedom with the Care Committee of the Nationwide Festival of Light, later to become 'Care Trust'. It was different in many ways from Pilot and they were keen to use it in conjunction with their own ministry. They were very helpful and a great encouragement to me. We had several meetings together, and people like Raymond Johnston, as Director of NFOL, introduced me to other well-known Christians interested in this subject. He also brought me into a Christian radio programme (called *Sunday Supplement*), which was all very daunting for a shy person like me, but I was learning to depend more on the Lord to give me confidence.

Gordon Landreth (then General Secretary of Evangelical Alliance) also heard about me and I was invited to take part in some discussions they were organising. These were between three evangelical Christians who supported homosexual relationships in certain situations and three who did not. I was introduced into the discussions after the initial meeting. This meant there were four contributors with personal experience of homosexuality, but I was the only one who believed that all homosexual sex was wrong. The atmosphere was good on the whole and I was impressed by the graciousness of all involved.

It was on this programme that I met Jean White, then Pastor of the London Metropolitan Community Church. She struck me as a warm, friendly and very 'homely' person, from a Brethren background, who believed that the Bible, and therefore God, approved of some homosexual relationships where love and commitment were involved. Tom Jones, another member of the group, talked about his own Methodist background and involvement in a long-term homosexual relationship. Tom also impressed me, but I could not agree with his viewpoint. Those of us who disagreed with Tom and Jean were surprised to admit, as we prayed together, that we had experienced Christian fellowship. I know this would be difficult for many to accept and it certainly was a surprise for me, until I realised that we are all guilty of compromising God's truth in some part of our lives, because we are all sinners. I still believed that people involved in homosexual relationships, no matter how stable or loving they may be, are disobeying God, but I could now understand how they had come to that point of view. Both Tom and

Jean had been badly hurt by misunderstanding Christians. They had each struggled against their homosexual feelings, then found so many of their needs for love and affirmation met through a gay and a lesbian relationship. Genital activity seemed for them a 'natural' expression of love. Such a measure of personal fulfilment can easily convince us that God is involved and therefore biblical disapproval for this is denied. The relevant texts are therefore assumed to not refer to monogamous homosexual relationships. I also became aware of other Christians who did not give the same authority to scripture. In a way I found their acceptance of homosexual relationships easier to understand because it was not based so strongly on biblical authority. Even so, just as many from an evangelical background have, like Tom and Jean, joined the so-call 'gay church', there are also those who come out of churches like MCC because they come to believe that their validation of some homosexual relationships is wrong.

These meetings were certainly an 'eye-opener' for me. They also introduced me to the Revd David Field, whose booklet *The Homosexual Way – A Christian Option?* helped me a lot at that time. David and his wife Margaret have since been a tremendous source of encouragement. Their God-given love, gentleness and humility are wonderful.

The meetings with the Care Committee of NFOL continued, but despite all the good intentions it did not seem to be possible to employ me along with Geoff. However, Roy Barker had been very much aware of all that was happening and was convinced that this area of ministry was right for me.

One Wednesday evening, when I was preparing to lock up the Church Hall, Roy asked how the talks with NFOL were going. He thought for a moment and said, 'I don't see why we can't start a ministry up here in the north. Let's see . . . we could set up a trust. Who would we need? A solicitor – yes, I can think of someone. A headmaster . . . yes. A treasurer . . . Martin, you contact Raymond and say that if they are not able to take you on, we can start something here. See what he says.'

I contacted Raymond who thought it was a great idea. 'Right!' Roy said when I told him, 'Come to the vicarage next Tuesday morning and we'll talk some more about this.'

I arrived at Roy's study, expecting a fairly brief talk with him about my future and the idea of a trust. His life was so full of meetings and appointments, in no way did I expect he would be able to spend much time with me at such short notice. How wrong I was. Miraculously, Roy always seemed to have the time whenever there was an urgent need for his ministry. We spent all morning and afternoon together, Barbara (Roy's wife) re-fuelling us with coffee and a snack for lunch. In that time, Roy had phoned all the people he saw as potential trustees and used his normal methods of persuasiveness. They all agreed and a meeting was arranged. A Council of Reference of those who agreed to have their names associated with the work was also created. A plan of action was made by Roy. A phone, office, leaflet, adverts, typewriter, filing cabinet and so on were itemised. I was given a list of tasks that I could do, including the wording for the leaflet. Roy felt that the True Freedom Trust should be something of an umbrella title, in case in the future other areas of ministry were brought in. He thought the teaching and counselling parts should be given separate names, to give us flexibility. Because of our very close links with Pilot and the vision for many Pilots around the country which had been discussed by the Care Committee, I assumed we could use the name 'Pilot' for the counselling ministry. We spent ages trying to think of a name that would link with Pilot for the teaching ministry. Originally, the reason for the name had been a nautical one – a ship in distress being led to safety by the pilot. The only linking word we could think of was 'chandler' (re-furbishing and equipping the ship). So it was decided – the ministries would be called Pilot and Chandler.

Roy wasted no time. When a letter appeared about homosexuality in the *Church Times* he responded, mentioned that two ministries existed, called Pilot and Chandler. This was even before the leaflet had been printed! It was just as well, because NFOL spotted the letter and graciously but understandably pointed out that if we were going to use the name Pilot then they should be involved in the trust and ministry, to some extent. They were quite right, of course. Roy and I did not feel this would be practical and would make the ministry very cumbersome. We wanted it to be northern based, for convenience, even though it would serve the whole country. We would therefore have to think of another name, which was very difficult. Since that time, I have come across many good names of similar ministries and wished I had thought of them first! Despite much thought and prayer, inspiration just did not come our way. Eventually, a music group at church whose name had been Harbinger (meaning 'messenger') split up. I liked the name and they agreed to let us use it. Some time afterwards I was amused to see one or two ex-members of the group wearing a T-shirt with 'Harbinger' emblazoned on the front. We wanted to retain the word 'Chandler' because Roy had already publicised it, if only in the *Church Times*.

It was decided that I would work from home and continue with my job at the Church Hall, until we had enough funds to pay my salary and a replacement had been found for my job at the church. We spent a long time preparing the leaflet and a booklet called *Homosexuality – An Explanation*. All our material would be printed by St Mary's own church press. I prepared the material and gave it to Roy, who then chopped, changed and condensed it. Eventually it was all set up and printed. Advertisements were put in many Christian papers and a letter sent to all local evangelical churches in the area, seeking support. The Trust Deed was signed on 29 June 1977. Once again, a great debt of gratitude was due to Roy for all his loving concern and wisdom. True Freedom Trust was now in operation and we awaited the response.

7
Growth of a Ministry

---◆---

INITIALLY, WE THOUGHT OF HAVING an office in Liverpool. One of our trustees owned a Christian Centre and there was a possibility of using one of the rooms. But this building was shortly sold so that venture did not materialise. However, we had already applied for a Post Office Box in the area and used this address in our advert and literature. The Post Office Box given us was No. 8 and the postal district of Liverpool 8. I hope it was not superstition, but considering my earlier experience with the number eight, I did wonder if the numbers chosen were a nice little humorous touch from the Lord!

The people from the Centre kindly collected the mail for me. However, travelling over to Liverpool from Upton was rather expensive, because of the Mersey Tunnel, which has a toll fee. So, after a few months we decided to move the PO Box to Upton and use the phone number of my home, given out discretely.

The initial adverts had been in the *Church Times*, *Crusade*, *Life of Faith*, *The Church of England Newspaper* and *Methodist Recorder*. We were obviously carefully vetted before being accepted by these publications for inclusion in the personal column. The original adverts read:

HOMOSEXUALITY –
Biblically-based counselling (Harbinger)/teaching (Chandler) ministries.
Free booklet – foolscap sae:
True Freedom Trust, PO Box 8, Liverpool L8 1YL.

Initially, many of the people responding to our adverts represented homosexual organisations seeking to find out where we stood. Occasionally there would be one or two strong comments, denouncing us and all we believed. Some clergy argued against us, especially on our stand for scriptural authority. Then there were many more people who wrote expressing appreciation that at last some Christians were taking a stand against homosexuality in the Church, but in a personal, pastoral and positive way. I was not inundated with mail at that time; it was more of a steady trickle. I kept thinking the Lord must have a strange sense of humour, giving me a ministry which consisted mainly of writing letters to people. This had always been quite an ordeal. I was so self-conscious about my layout and grammar, wondering what people might think of me. The most difficult letters of course were the replies to people struggling with homosexual problems. They were nearly all Christians. Some had never shared their difficulties with anyone else before. I realised very early on that I would have to devise a simple form of coding that would preserve anonymity, just in case anyone broke into my house and tried blackmail. It was very unlikely that anyone would know where I lived, but I wanted to be able to assure people who contacted us of very strict confidentiality, which is vital in this kind of ministry, as in any other. This need had been highlighted for me when I worked for the Samaritans: their own filing system and confidentiality had impressed me tremendously.

I therefore devised a system of coding which meant that none of the letters sent or other confidences given by people could be linked with their names and addresses. Only people directly involved in the ministry of T*f*T would know who had contacted us for help. I just had to make sure that I could understand my own coding system!

I found it very difficult to answer the pleas for help from Christians struggling with homosexuality. I was only too aware from past experience how easily I could be misunderstood, or sound very trite and unsympathetic. Quite a lot of prayer was also needed as I struggled with my grammar for each letter, sitting at the old oak desk in my bedroom, gazing from the window into my garden below and the backs of the modern semis beyond. I had bought a Burmese cat by this time, who was completely dependent on me, following everywhere I went and jumping on my lap at the slightest opportunity. Misty was small, slim and grey with specks of cream. She also talked a lot and at this early time of her life often made a lot of noise! In a way it was a comfort to me, as I sat with a letter in front of me, poised at the typewriter with Misty on my lap. Some-

Growth of a Ministry

times it seemed that her gentle murmurings were joining me in prayer for inspiration! I decided it was best to express some of my fears and anxieties to the recipient of the letter, in a way to prepare him or her for any misinterpretation. I still do this and ask the person to respond with any questions, comments or criticisms. I found in this way it was possible to strike up quite a relationship with someone through a letter. Even when I gave my phone number, very few people were prepared to use it. Letters somehow seemed safer. None of my correspondents lived locally. Even today, in our e-mail groups, we often find people share more about themselves than in the face-to-face groups.

Eventually, someone did decide to come and see me, all the way from London. At first it was only going to be for a day visit, but I gave him the option of staying overnight, if he wished. So many feelings went through my mind as I waited for him to arrive at the railway station. Imagine coming all the way from London to see me! What was he expecting? Would he be disappointed?

The arrangements for meeting amused me a little, but there was also a sense in which they reminded me of my 'degenerate days' and I wondered if it was right to think it funny.

'How will I know you?'

'I will be wearing a blue anorak. I'm tall, dark and . . . bald!'

Once we met only the fears of his expectations remained. He already knew something of my story, so I decided I must initially listen carefully to what he was and was not saying. Occasionally I would encourage him to talk by making it clear that I understood most of what happens in the homosexual scene. I therefore would not be shocked by any of his revelations. My ideology of the homosexual's basic search for love was being confirmed – he was a man desperately searching for love and longing to be able to find it in the heterosexual Christian world, but somehow unable to do so. No matter how many times he tried to grit his teeth and overcome his homosexual feelings, he would slip into homosexual bars and other meeting places, not necessarily making any social contact, but feeling accepted and loved when surrounded by others with homosexual feelings. In keeping with many others who were to visit me, this man said that I was the first Christian he had met who experienced homosexual feelings and yet was not involved in a homosexual lifestyle. Eventually he decided that he would stay overnight and travel back the next morning. As we talked, various needs in his life were highlighted, and I could see how God could well want them to be met, but it was not easy. It would mean making himself very vulnerable to other Christians – and what would happen if they did not respond? How could I possibly guarantee that they would understand? Most people contacting us, having not shared their difficulties with other Christians, are fairly convinced they will be misunderstood and rejected. Such rejection may not be in terms of a positive decision or verbalised statement. It is more likely to be a much more subtle rejection, often not recognised as such by the person guilty of it. Even today, I find myself at fault in this area in regard to my attitude to my old gay friends. Because I find I cannot identify with them and sometimes even feel uncomfortable in their company for many different reasons, I avoid the situation and make few steps towards them. I may not want to admit that I have rejected them, but in fact I have done just that.

Some Christians, because of their lack of real understanding of the homosexual person, plus a misinterpretation of the biblical references, make a much more positive decision to reject. They decide that they will not even 'eat with such a person'. The reasoning behind this stems from some words of the Apostle Paul to Christians in Corinth: 'But now I am writing to you that you must not associate with anyone who calls himself a brother but is sexually immoral or greedy, an idolater or a slanderer, a drunkard or a swindler. With such a man do not even eat' (1 Cor. 5:11). These are difficult verses, but they are not referring to someone seeking to overcome a particular sin, but rather a Christian who actually accepts sinful behaviour and perhaps 'they not only continue to do these very things but also approve of those who practise them' (Rom. 1:32b). With such a person a Christian is not to have intimate fellowship, partly, I feel sure, to encourage the person to see what is wrong. Paul is therefore not referring to someone struggling with homosexual feelings and temptations. I have rarely seen church discipline exercised in this 'biblical way'. It is usually an act of punishing the sinner, who already feels devastated by the guilt of his sin. The action of the church fellowship involved is therefore, in some ways, anti-Christian, because it denies the Cross of Christ to bring forgiveness and redemption.

There is sometimes even a failure among Christians to recognise that homosexual feelings or orientation are not a personal choice, although putting them into practice, of course, is. Most importantly, it must be realised that the sexually immoral person is not mentioned in isolation. An idolater, slanderer, drunkard, swindler or greedy person is also to be treated in the same way. Can any of us really say we have never been guilty of any of these sins? I am sure many of us have been guilty and unrepentant, at times. The Evangelical Sisters of Mary helped me to realise that even my anxiety at what others might think of me can often lead to pride, which is a form of idolatry.

Many Christians have been greatly hurt by this type of unbiblical judgementalism. I began to find that some of the people who contacted me believed that even a homosexual orientation is wrong in God's eyes. It was a wonderful experience to know of the joy and relief felt by them, when we opened up God's Word and saw that it is only homosexual acts that are condemned in scripture. I was amazed by the number of Christians with homosexual feelings who had never knowingly met another homosexual, let alone been involved in sexual activity. In that sense, they couldn't identify with my experience, but, as the ministry grew, they would soon meet others with a similar story.

Some of the people contacting me live a kind of double existence; on the one hand being very involved with Christian fellowship, but then slipping into homosexual activity compulsively – usually the anonymous type of one-off sexual encounters, experiencing a sudden giving in to temptation, followed, of course, by tremendous guilt. Pornography is a big problem for many Christians, including those with no experience of homosexual relationships – the Internet of course now being a major source. It is a private world and a seemingly intimate one of fascination and excitement. Of course it isn't really as private as one hopes. Pornography soon becomes an addiction, once sexual pleasure has been gained from it. Before the World Wide Web almost every magazine stand could be a fascination and cause real temptation. Homosexual pornography was not as readily available as its heterosexual counterpart, but in some ways that made the search for it a compulsive, soul-destroying drive. Again and again the same story would be told: 'I pick up the pornography, use it perhaps once or twice, feel disgusted with myself and destroy it. Then I find myself in the shop again . . .' Such excitement has now become much more accessible through the computer. Gay chatrooms and porn of every conceivable type are available on-line.

In my early days as a Christian I would have thought, if not said, 'The answer to these sorts of problems is easy – claim the Lord's victory and fight the temptation in the strength of that victory.' Praise the Lord, that for some it really is just as straightforward as that. But I was now thankful that God allowed me to experience difficulties and problems of one sort and another (and still does) because this enabled me to identify with so many of the desperately hurting people who were contacting me. I felt I could share something of Paul's experience:

> Praise be to the God and Father of our Lord Jesus Christ, the Father of compassion and the God of all comfort, who comforts us in all our troubles, so that we can comfort those in any trouble with the comfort we ourselves have received from God. For just as the sufferings of Christ flow over into our lives, so also through Christ our comfort overflows. If we are distressed, it is for your comfort and salvation; if we are comforted, it is for your comfort, which produces in you patient endurance of the same sufferings we suffer. And our hope for you is firm, because we know that just as you share in our sufferings, so also you share in our comfort.
> (2 Cor. 1:3–7)

I always find these verses tremendously encouraging. They help to give a positive reason for present and past problems, trials and difficulties of all sorts.

My personal experiences were beginning to have some purpose for my present ministry. God was using me, not despite of all I have been and am today, but because of it. I was able to share this with others seeking my help – I hope not as a glib answer to their problems, but at least as some measure of encouragement. Many of these hurting people had such a low self-image. They felt 'dirty' and 'abnormal', longing to have heterosexual feelings 'like everyone else'. My experiences in Upton, especially with one or two women I knew, encouraged me to ask those coming to see me if they appreciated that heterosexual people often have sexual problems too. Inevitably, the reply would be, 'Do they really? I suppose they must have . . . I wish I had heterosexual problems, at least they're normal.'

I had been blessed in many ways through my relationships with

Tim and John. But I soon realised that for some of the Christians I was meeting in T*f*T, such intimacy seemed out of the question. They were fearful of becoming sexually attracted to anyone of the same sex they grew close to. They were fearful of sharing their problems with others, in case they were rejected. They were fearful of a lonely old age and sometimes they even feared their salvation had been lost.

'There is no fear in love. But perfect love drives out fear, because fear has to do with punishment. The one who fears is not made perfect in love' (1 John 4:18). How I longed to help these men and women grow more towards being 'made perfect in love'. How I longed to experience more of that in my own life. In these early days, I was beginning to see beneath the 'presenting problems' to the underlying needs that God wanted to meet. In many situations I felt able to suggest ways in which God could meet these needs – but it was always within the context of the Body of Christ (the Church). Nearly every time I had the frustration of seeing how God could bring fulfilment and joy to a person's life, knowing full well that it would be unlikely the Church would meet his or her needs. While this was primarily a failing in the fellowship, the person concerned would often be unprepared to take the risk of finding the necessary love within the Body of Christ. If you are convinced you are not lovable and will therefore not be loved by others, you tend to wait for them to make the first move towards you. This is certainly my experience. But it is a vicious circle, because others then feel you do not want them, your low self-image having made you withdraw behind a mask. You therefore drive away the very love for which you long.

At this stage of my ministry I did not delve much into the reasons for the lack of self-love. The priority seemed more and more to help the churches become better places in which hurting people could come to know the healing power of God's love being expressed through his people. This meant much more teaching about sensitive subjects like homosexuality, so that people with problems would know they were understood, loved and accepted. It also meant more teaching about loving one another in Christ.

I found I was seeking to provide something of the love and encouragement that should have been coming from the Church. It was a tremendous privilege to share in the deepest secrets of a person's life. To hear someone say, 'I have never told this to anyone else before' is a truly moving experience. Many felt a tremendous burden lifted by simply sharing, for the first time in a completely honest way, with someone they felt understood them. I was staggered to know how far people would travel, just to be able to do this. It was quite common for someone to come from the other end of the country. In many cases they would even be unable to stay overnight and travelled back the same day. It was always daunting – I feared they were expecting too much. Sometimes I almost wished I could pay their train fare so they would not be too disappointed. Thankfully, no one actually felt they had wasted their money, although the Lord had not always ministered in the way they expected. So often it was imagined that one visit to me would suddenly turn them into heterosexuals!

The people I found most difficult to deal with were those who had become disillusioned with evangelical Christians. Often they had been prayed with, anointed and 'delivered' – but with still no change from their homosexual feelings. There was sometimes a temporary absence of sexual thoughts when experiencing the power of the Holy Spirit, but it was not sustained. I did not find this difficult to understand. After all, if one is suddenly overwhelmed by the love and power of God, sexual thoughts are unlikely to be at the forefront of the mind. Sometimes, it seems especially for women, the experience of being filled with the Holy Spirit takes the lid off deeply buried emotions. The result can actually be an awareness of homosexual feelings, perhaps for the first time in the person's life. It seemed many people had a somewhat naive idea that sexual feelings could be switched off through ministry, and then remain off for the rest of one's life. Surely many influences affect our sexual desires – circumstances, people, self-worth, physical and mental illness, and so on.

As more people began contacting us for help and church leaders were seeking more information and advice, the financial support of the ministry increased. Only a couple of people were covenanting or giving on a regular basis, but the commitment was growing. We hoped it would not be too long before I was able to relinquish my job at the Church Hall and work for T*f*T full-time. I was obviously restricted in terms of time spent outside the parish. One or two speaking engagements were beginning to appear. This vital part of our ministry was the most daunting for me. I remember going to Southampton University, having been invited by Eddy Stride's son,

Stephen. He was a good-looking young man with a mass of fair, curly hair and a warm, friendly, effervescent character. It was so exhilarating to be with him. His enthusiasm to share the Gospel was balanced with a warmth and desire to understand. He did not seem threatened in any way or nervous when in the company of a homosexual at the college, who I noticed quite blatantly made several verbal 'passes' at him, in terms of comments about his good looks.

Despite all this I was tremendously nervous and phoned John to ask him to pray for me. It seemed quite likely that there would be at least some opposition. The meeting hall was very large and smartly designed, with seating in the form of broad carpeted steps. As Stephen and I watched the students arriving, he would say, 'Oh he's from the Gay Soc – a really militant guy. He's a Marxist . . .' and so on. I tried to retain some composure. I decided that one of the main reasons for my nerves was the fear of looking stupid – making a fool of myself.

This was really pride (remembering my Canaan experience!). I struggled to give it to the Lord and allow myself to feel secure in him. All I can say is that the Holy Spirit really did take control and once the meeting was under way, I was amazed at myself. I felt I should start by sharing something of my apprehensions and fears, knowing how I expected the gay militant to respond. I was amazed at their reaction. There was more respect, even if they disagreed, than I anticipated. Oh that more Christians could have Stephen's zeal and enthusiasm!

Needless to say, the response from churches was very poor indeed. Less than a handful of local churches responded, even though Roy Barker had written nearly 200 letters.

There was now to be a change in the situation at home, which greatly affected the course of our ministry. Since my mother's death, father lived on his own in Liverpool and obviously felt lonely. He used to come over once a week on my day off, or I would travel over to Liverpool. He raised the idea of us moving in together, which I resisted at first but then thought it could work if we had two living rooms so that I could entertain my friends without it interfering with him. We eventually found a pre-war detached house in Upton, which had remained empty for many years and had not been decorated since 1949! It needed a lot of money spending on it, but had great potential. The large rear garden had woodland at the end and was not overlooked. Although it only had three bedrooms, it seemed to be full of small rooms – larders, cloak rooms, wash rooms and storage rooms. We managed to persuade the owner to sell it and set to work with renovations. The Lord's hand could clearly be seen in the whole situation, partly because of the ease with which we had sold our own modern houses. My only regret, later, was that we had not done more internal structural alterations, knocking some of the rooms together and making a better kitchen. We managed with a very small, fairly old-fashioned kitchen and a morning-room. I know my mother would not have approved, but I think in some ways the smaller old-fashioned rooms, morning-room and larder reminded father of bygone days. It was not easy readjusting to living with one's parent, after so many years 'out of the nest'. I also found myself reluctant to share many things with my father, possibly because this had become a 'natural' reaction when I was involved in a gay lifestyle. He adapted wonderfully, however, and it was a great joy to see him moving on spiritually. I am sure this work of the Holy Spirit in his life started primarily after my mother died, although there had always been a 'simple faith' there since his childhood days as a choirboy in the West Country town of Shepton Mallet. However, I found it difficult to honestly share my thoughts and feelings with my father, and this continued to bother me. When we worked together in the bakery and I enjoyed buying new cars, we seemed to have plenty to talk about. I was now finding it difficult on my own with him and often felt guilty that I longed for my former independence. Since my mother died, it seemed I had now become my father's reason for living and the most important person in his life. I often wondered if this is how my mother had sometimes felt. I remember her saying once that she wished he would join a gardening club or go out with some of his male friends.

Meanwhile at church we had built a large extension, because the original Victorian building was too small for the congregation. There had also been a refurbishing of the Church Halls, through a job-creation scheme. One of the leaders of this, a qualified joiner, was offered the job of full-time maintenance man and Hallkeeper. This was an answer to prayer and a fulfilment of Roy's vision. My caretaking at the Church Hall had only been thought of as a temporary measure, even though it lasted for nearly four years. It was now obviously the right time to take the step of faith and work for

T*f*T full-time. In February 1978, I became the self-employed staff worker of T*f*T, being paid fifteen pounds per week by the Trust, plus a five-pound retainer by the church, for some part-time verging duties.

My father's standard of living, as far as food goes, was completely different from my own, and I could not afford to keep up with it. He very generously agreed to subsidise me in this way as part of his support for my ministry. I guess he found his own ministry in feeding me and the guests who came to stay, usually for counselling.

At first I found it very difficult to adjust to the new work routine. I felt guilty if I was not actually doing something physically for T*f*T. I had been conditioned that working for wages involved manual activity. Reading, thinking and even praying, did not seem like work. I guess this must be a common problem for people coming into full-time Christian work from a manual occupation. We had the phone transferred from my other house and used exclusively as a T*f*T phone, in my little office at home. There was just enough room for a desk and a chair, which faced the window, looking out on the long garden. My only storage space consisted of an old kitchen cupboard, which just fitted on the back wall, and two wide shelves on the other walls. The rough brickwork and simple hardboard-lined roof meant there were regular showers of brick dust! However, my determination to have my own office (there was no room for anyone else, anyway) rather than working from a bedroom made it all seem worthwhile, at first. I attempted to convert my bedroom into a bed-sitting room, by trying to make the bed look like a sofa and putting two comfy chairs at 45 degrees at the other end of the room. I thought I had succeeded, until much later a couple of people, now friends, remarked at their surprise and alarm when they first met me and I took them to my bedroom!

Roy was always keen on 'door knocking'. It was one of the reasons his ministry in Upton had been so blessed by the Lord. Now he was convinced this was also essential for T*f*T; the difference being that I would not be knocking on the doors of householders, but vicars and pastors. Visiting as a lay minister had given me some experience in this field, but I always hated going out on my own. Now I had to face this and another problem as well. It did not take me long to realise that the pastors and vicars were often very suspicious, or at least uneasy, about my theological stand. I could feel them scrutinising me mentally, as I shared what I believed God said about homosexuality and the basis and vision of the ministry. After a while there would be a release of this tension and I was often made to feel very much at home. Sometimes I was even invited in for a meal. However, every time I approached the idea of raising the subject in church, there were tremendous reservations. 'I don't think the elders would approve. It's too delicate a subject.'

'I don't think we have anyone with this problem in our church, but we will know where to come if we do come across anybody. Could we contact you?'

I would try to point out that not only may some of their congregation have homosexual feelings, but the much wider implications raised by this subject are relevant and important for all Christians. This did not seem to impress them. Several attempts at door-knocking on local evangelical leaders' doors failed to produce even one speaking engagement. I plucked up courage and phoned a few local church leaders who were not known to be evangelicals. I had some varied responses:

'I am not sure that we have what you would term a fellowship, but I am interested in your point of view.'

'I am absolutely amazed that anyone can believe what you believe. I would happily bless a couple of men or women, if they asked me. I've never met anyone who believes in the Genesis story!'

However, despite all this negative response, speaking engagements were beginning to happen: I was given invitations by a couple of theological colleges – Oak Hill College, London and Trinity College, Bristol. At first these were tremendously daunting for a non-academic like me. When students and staff would chat beforehand and mention 'my lecture', I frequently felt like saying, 'I don't lecture really, you know, I'm not clever enough. I just talk and share.'

After the session, much to my amazement, students and even some of the lecturers showed a lot of interest and treated me with much respect and admiration. I was just beginning to realise that Christian academics, whom I used to find very threatening, were vulnerable human beings themselves. This point was driven home to me even more forcibly when they started to come for personal help and advice.

A few invitations came from universities and colleges, mainly through the Christian Unions, which was encouraging. I was certainly gaining a little more self-confidence, but on every occasion I had to surrender to Christ my fear of looking stupid and my desire to impress.

I especially remember two meetings where there was some opposition. The first was at Liverpool University and had been organised by John. I opened up by saying that if anyone had told me six years ago I would be addressing a Christian meeting on this subject, I would have thought they were crazy. I shared my shyness and homosexual background. There were a couple of people in the audience who had known me slightly in my days on the 'gay scene'. One commented afterwards, 'I have listened to everything you said this evening and the only thing I agree with is what you said at the very beginning about never believing this would be possible for you.' The other meeting had been organised by the Festival of Light and was held in a meeting room over shops in Regent Street, London. The room was packed with people and David Field was the speaker. I joined him on the platform, with Eddy Stride and Edward Shackleton. It was an intimate atmosphere inasmuch as the audience were tightly packed and very close to the platform.

As I glanced towards them, waiting for David to speak, it was very obvious that many of them were likely to be fairly militant. The atmosphere that made me believe this is difficult to describe. In some ways they seemed already angry and impatient, perhaps even like defiant children, determined to shock and offend. I could feel the tension and nerves in the pit of my stomach. What was I going to be expected to do and say?

David started speaking and immediately there were heckles and comments. It was very difficult, if not impossible to hear what David was saying. Because of the relatively small size of the room, there was no amplification. It became even noisier and a group of people near the front started to tear out pages from a large family Bible and throw them at the stage. Eddy Stride kept telling David to continue speaking from his notes, because the talk was being recorded. I guess it was thought that David was close enough to the recorder's microphone to prevent any other noises drowning him on the tape, but it seemed a bizarre situation. Some wondered if the meeting should be stopped, but that would be admitting defeat. If the people causing the disturbance refused to leave or be quiet it would again be playing into their hands to either force them out or call the police. There had already been an ugly incident in All Soul's Church, involving some gay Christians, which attracted publicity. The audience (mainly the militants that is) demanded a time for questions. A few people pointed at me and said, in a rather mocking tone, 'We want to know what you do to gay people on Merseyside?' It reminded me of the 'cages' from my brief boarding school days. I tried to be as positive and sensitive as possible. I explained where most of the people in touch with us stood and that many had contacted organisations agreeing with their point of view, rather than ours, but found they were unable to help. I can't remember much else of what I shared that evening, but I was aware, as never before, of a special anointing from the Lord. At one stage a woman called out, 'Why don't you send us all to the gas chambers? That's what you really want!' To my utter amazement I shouted back, 'If the day that happens ever arrives, then I will be first in the queue for the gas chamber!' Looking back, I am not sure if that was the wisest comment to make!

Afterwards a number of people from organisations who support some types of homosexual relationships within the Church came up to David, saying they did not want to be associated with the more militant members of the audience.

I found that experiences like this one have left me with a sense of feeling threatened, when in the company of people involved in a gay lifestyle. I tend to assume they hate me, because they believe that Christians like myself strongly disapprove of them. The feelings of fear and anger that come across at meetings like this one have obviously not left me completely unscarred, emotionally. I never cease to admire those Christians who constantly have to suffer that sort of opposition because of their faith. I know the coward in me would make me want to run a mile, even though I know God always comes to our rescue. I guess it is a problem I have with confrontation.

8
Crisis of Faith – What Does the Bible Say?

THE MINISTRY WAS NOW QUITE WELL ESTABLISHED and although many Christians and church fellowships were reluctant to support T*f*T as perhaps they would other societies, there were some very committed people behind us. Financially, there was not enough regular or covenanted giving to pay my salary, but the Lord provided for all our financial needs. We often wondered if we should take a further step of faith and spend money we did not have, expecting the Lord to provide it. In our situation this seemed wrong until there was very clear guidance from God. I was beginning to enjoy talking to Christian groups and was gaining more confidence.

Then, early in 1979, I read a book from America by two Christian women from an evangelical background. Neither apparently homosexual. They came down on the side of supporting homosexual relationships in certain situations. Many of their arguments were not new to me. They were basically echoing what the more 'liberal' theologians were saying, but it was dressed up in evangelical terminology. The two main points which impressed me were their arguments against the hurt and prejudice shown by many Christians and churches (having seen something of this), and the fact that they were not homosexual themselves and therefore seemingly unbiased.

Needless to say, reading this book left me very unsettled and insecure. I was not convinced they were right, but still wondered if I could be wrong. Up to this point I tended to accept much of what I was reading on the subject of homosexuality, because I agreed and could understand the strong biblical basis on which it was all founded. Perhaps I had not really thought it all through thoroughly for myself. But now I felt lonely and frightened, especially as I was due to make my second or third visit to Oak Hill College in two days. What on earth was I going to say? How could I speak with a strong sense of conviction? I dreaded the thought of it, but knew I must phone David Field and tell him how I was feeling. We would probably have to cancel this visit, but what about the future of T*f*T? How many people would I be letting down?

David was marvellous – he said that he understood and would like me to come and speak to his students anyway. 'Just share how you feel with them', he said. David asked me to say more about my doubts and uncertainties. In his soft, gentle voice he graciously shared that he knew the book in question. He felt himself they were really echoing what John McNeil (the Roman Catholic author) had said. Apparently their translation of the Greek words in the relevant verses was not at all accurate (David was teaching New Testament Greek so he knew about such things!). What encouraged me most of all in David's attitude were his words, 'Martin, all I can say is that every time I read a new book published on this subject I pray that I may be convinced that my views are wrong. I have seen some of the agony experienced by Christians with homosexual feelings. However, this book did not convince me my views were wrong at all.' Since that time, both David and I have seen something more of what God can do in terms of positive help and healing. It may be that he would add something a little more positive, today.

Before going to Oak Hill I also went to see a Christian student friend in York, who had homosexual feelings. He was firm and positive with me. I could imagine myself telling someone else what he was saying to me! He was so loving and concerned that he phoned me at Tim's sister's house, where I was staying before I went to Oak Hill, simply to say that he and one or two others were praying for me. His love and concern meant so much.

Over these few days I had been forced into doing a lot of thinking and praying. Eventually, just in time for my visit to Oak Hill, I felt more positive and secure in my beliefs. This had been a painful but necessary experience. It helped me to see how easily convinced someone with strong homosexual feelings could be by the arguments of a more liberal theology, when expressed by a Christian claiming to believe in the authority of scripture. Understanding what God is saying to us today, through his Word the Bible, is a lifelong process. I remember meeting a well-known Bible teacher, a retired bishop, who said, 'It never ceases to amaze me how much more I have to learn about the wonders of God's Word!' I replied, 'Wow, if you think that, where does that leave the likes of me!' So, yes I'm still learning, especially in the area of the Bible and sexuality. Looking at the passages relevant to the homosexual issue has also made me realise how much we depend on the translators of the original texts. This is especially true in the case of 1 Corinthians 6. If I want to check out a new translation I usually go to that chapter and see what it says. If I don't believe it has it right, I tend to lose faith in the rest of the translation – probably totally unfairly!

What do I believe the Bible says about homosexuality? First, it must be said that the Bible does not know or say anything about sexual orientation. In other words, biblically there is no such person as a homosexual or heterosexual. That thinking and terminology only began in the nineteenth century. I wonder if this actually handicaps us, in some ways, in our modern-day thinking of God's view of sexuality? I believe we also need to recognise that God's original intention or ideal was radically changed when mankind disobeyed him at the Fall. We don't have a lot of pre-Fall information, but it does seem our lives were intended to be radically different from what we accept as the 'norm' today. For example, it would appear from what we read in the first chapters of Genesis, that before the Fall there would have been no 'toil', no pain in childbirth and no old age and death. In terms of sex, I wonder if the fact that the man and woman were only aware of their nakedness, in particular their genitals, after the Fall means there was a sexual purity, far from our experience today? Maybe there was not even a sexual attraction as we understand it today? Perhaps it was only experienced by the one man for the one woman and vice versa, within their marriage. So Adam was an 'evesexual' and Eve an 'adamsexual'. Their bodies were clearly designed for each other as opposite or 'hetero' genders, but in a very different way from the way we define or usually express 'heterosexuality' today. In other words, in the context of the Fall is it helpful to use words today such as 'normal', when clearly all sexuality is 'deviant' or 'abnormal' in terms of God's original ideal or definition of 'normality'? The impression often given is that God is happier with sexual attraction towards someone of the opposite sex, who is not one's marriage partner, than he is with sexual attraction towards the same sex. The former is usually regarded as 'normal' and the latter 'abnormal'. I am not convinced that this way of thinking is helpful or biblical. Encouraging someone to see themselves as 'abnormal', in contrast to others who are 'normal', does not encourage wholeness and the right kind of self-acceptance. I prefer to see myself, including my sexuality, just like everyone else – 'normally abnormal' as far as God's ideal is concerned.

From this basis, I can now begin to understand what is acceptable to God in terms of sex and what is not, recognising the limits of my 'fallenness'. I believe scripture has made the fundamental prohibition very clear. That is, any sex between two people outside the marriage of a man and woman offends God and his standard of holiness for his people. That provokes many questions. For example, why should that be, when love is being expressed between two people of the same sex? Again, should the search for healing mean helping everyone experience sexual attraction for the opposite sex? In scripture is not healing defined as 'wholeness'? A sense of experiencing my value, purpose and meaning to my life in a relationship with God is one way, albeit inadequately, I try to define wholeness. Perhaps, therefore, healing is the process of dealing with all that obstructs these 'whole' relationships involving God, myself and others.

Trying to understand why God is offended by any sex outside marriage is not easy. I get frustrated reading books on homosexuality which quote statistics seeking to prove that men involved in homosexuality are less likely to live long and often contract sexually transmitted diseases. The aim seems to be an attempt to prove that God is offended by homosexuality because it will harm us. Women are usually left out of this argument, because I think lesbian sex is probably the lowest risk behaviour, and their relationships often last much longer than their male counterparts and possibly even many married ones. If the statistics often quoted are intended to give a reason for the biblical prohibition, they fail miserably in my opinion. I'm also unsure about the reliability of statistics about sexual behaviour, because of their limited scope in terms of people who are prepared to be involved.

I wonder if the reason for God's prohibition of sex outside marriage is more related to his original, that is 'pre-Fall', intention for the mystery of the one flesh relationship. We know the human sexual act is very different from its animal counterparts. It involves a level of stimulation and excitement, necessary for its function, not found in sex between animals. I don't believe this was simply for procreation, but maybe even more so for pleasure. Perhaps, looking at the creation narrative in Genesis 2, it was also intended to be an act of worship? That is, mankind celebrating and remembering the very act of God's Creation. I wonder if this is a vital part of the 'holiness' that God wants us to experience in order that we may be 'holy as he is holy'? This is holiness that is a way of describing an obedience to God's will, rather than the self-righteous way it is often perceived. It means God's people live and behave in a distinctly different way from the rest of his creation. This symbolic mystery of a 'one flesh' sexual act may therefore be partly intended as a celebration of humankind's creation. This, to me, seems to explain why any sex outside this ideal offends God, as does any act of 'unholiness' or disobedience. Although, since the Fall, we have all been tempted and fall prey to unholy behaviour, even as disobedient little children, God's ideal and his standards have remained. They are something for which we are all expected to attain, even though we continually fail.

Having established how I believe scripture condemns any sex outside marriage between a man and woman, and why I believe that is so, now let's look at the specific texts relating to homosexuality. Starting in Genesis, I do not believe the story of Sodom gives a fair picture of God's view of homosexuality, because it talks of attempted sexual abuse rather than a loving relationship. There were also other sins of Sodom which included a lack of concern for the poor and needy in their society (Ezekiel 16:48–9).

Leviticus says a lot about ritual and symbolism which may not seem relevant to our modern culture, although there are also many references to God's holiness and his desire that we should be holy, too. The sexual examples of unholiness include incest, bestiality, adultery and 'a man lying with another man as if he were a woman' (Leviticus 18:22). I used to wonder if these verses in Leviticus really were relevant for us today, in the light of some Levitical prohibitions, like the wearing of mixed fabrics. But I had failed to appreciate how important are the standards of Godly behaviour listed in Leviticus and how much the rest of scripture, including Jesus' and Paul's teaching, are influenced by them.

In Matthew 19:11–12 we see Jesus telling his disciples, with I guess some Pharisees listening in, that there will be many different situations in which someone may be unmarried. Only one of these seems to be by choice, for the sake of God's Kingdom. I wonder if the terminology Jesus uses is encompassing every type of human situation which accounts for a person being unmarried? These would include physical, emotional, circumstantial and maybe sexual reasons. Modern terminology would probably express these things differently, and that would certainly be true in the case of sexual orientation – a modern concept in itself, as I said earlier. We know that Jesus' description of an unmarried person as a 'eunuch' would not necessarily mean someone castrated, but someone who is celibate. So Jesus is saying, if you are not married, you are celibate. In accordance with the teaching of the Old Testament, Jesus was affirming there should be no sex outside marriage. He wouldn't have needed to unwrap or explain it. He was simply echoing familiar and accepted Jewish teaching, as from God.

Some of the examples or reasons Jesus shares for a person being unmarried may also give some insight into the possible roots of homosexual issues. This may be drawing too much from the words he uses, but terms like 'born that way' or 'made that way by men' may be intended to encompass every situation in which a person is unmarried.

We know that from the moment of conception we are receiving 'messages' from our environment, circumstances and human relationships. Some are messages directly given by other people and others are interpretations by us from whatever we are experiencing. Some of what we are believing will be true and some false or a lie. The most important influences in this development of our own unique self-belief system will be our parents or parental role models. The parent or role model of the same sex is an especially important influence in the development of our self-worth. The 'messages' about ourselves we receive from this person or prominent role model are often especially significant. Ideally they should be very positive ones – 'You're safe . . . You don't have to be different, to be loved and valued by me . . .' Of course many other factors can influence the way we receive or don't receive this kind of affirmation. We can refuse to accept it, for one reason or another. Or circumstances may make it difficult to receive or hear it. Or the messages themselves may be drowned by louder affirmations from another source or person. There could even be some genetic influences that help to prevent the affirmation being received and believed by us. Everyone's experience of these vital factors in our self-image building will be different, as will be our responses. However, some of us who believe as children we are not all we could or ought to be, will find this affecting our early peer group relationships. The need to find my sense of worth and value through another of the same sex will continue, and for some, but not all, will become in part a sexual attraction or desire. This will often mean the person of the same sex to whom I am attracted is the 'person I would like to be' or the 'person I would like to have been'. In other words there is a link, often subtle, between my sense of 'self-worth' and the way that has been formed, and my same-sex attractions and desires.

This is not intended as a definitive blueprint for the way in which sexual attractions develop, but points to some common factors often present. It also helps to explain why our sexual feelings sometimes change at different times in our lives. Some people find, as the same-sex needs diminish and self-worth increases, that relationships with the opposite sex may become more obviously sexual. Others with strong sexual desires for the opposite sex find they unexpectedly, for the first time, experience similar sexual desires for someone of the same sex. An unmet same-sex need from childhood surfaces in a present-day relationship and, often to the horror of the person concerned, has become erotic. Therefore, none of us can say for sure we will never have homosexual or heterosexual feelings. We are all an incredibly complex mixture of circumstances and influences that have made us feel about ourselves and others the way we do today. Likewise, because so many factors are involved in the development of our sexuality, we should not assume that one person, relationship or circumstance is entirely responsible for anyone's sexuality. I believe this whole developmental process, and its effects, can give us a deeper understanding of ourselves and others. It is therefore an important part of our value, a catalyst for our growth and a way in which we find more of God's love. That's why I can thank God for my sexuality and my ministry through it.

Returning to scripture, the Apostle Paul reminds us in Romans 1:18–2:1 that male and female same-sex behaviour is one example, among many, of humankind's disobedience to a holy God. The words translated as 'natural' and 'unnatural' are relating to God's perfect nature and design for his creation, not what is natural for us. Some argue that Paul is referring to heterosexuals involved in homosexuality, as unnatural for them, but not for homosexuals. I strongly disagree with this in view of the whole context of Romans 1. In any case, even if this was so, Paul describes the homosexual behaviour itself as 'shameful', which would suggest he means whatever the circumstance. I believe Paul is showing us, as humankind, that we have all 'exchanged the truth of God for a lie and worshipped and served created things, rather than the Creator'. In other words, we have all sinned. Romans has been described as a wonderful exposition of the Gospel. It therefore makes sense that Paul should start it by showing us why we need the Gospel. I wonder if Paul was influenced by Leviticus in his other examples of disobedient behaviour which include disobedient children, gossip and envy.

In 1 Corinthians 6:9–11, Paul mentions behaviour and the resultant lifestyle choice that is not compatible with God's Kingdom. He highlights the greedy, idolaters, revilers, adulterers and then uses two Greek words, which are it seems not easy to translate accurately. One word (*arsenokoites*) seems to have been borrowed by Paul from the Greek translation of Leviticus 18. It is literally describing the behaviour of a man who is lying with another man as if the other was a woman. This behaviour would not have been viewed negatively by many in the Corinthian culture, as the man taking this active role would have been regarded as quite 'macho'. Then Paul also uses a word (*malakos*) to describe the behaviour of the more passive partner in this relationship. This behaviour and the person involved in it would have been ridiculed and condemned by the Corinthians. It and he would have been seen as 'unmanly'. In some translations both words are translated together as homosexual perverts. The New International Version translates them as 'homosexual offenders' and 'male prostitutes', which I don't believe is really accurate. Then Paul reminds the Corinthian Christians they have made a lifestyle choice to no longer live in this way. He also speaks, in a very dynamic way, of their redemption – 'you were washed, sanctified and justified'. These are very powerful theological terms of redemption. He goes on to give his statement, and their experience of sanctification, tremendous authority by adding – 'In the name of the Lord Jesus Christ and by the Spirit of our God'. His words are not addressing their struggle with sin or the lack of it – they affirm their redemption. The inclusion of those involved in passive homosexual behaviour would have been remarkable for the Corinthians to hear – the very opposite of a homophobic statement and culturally extraordinary.

Wherever same-sex behaviour is mentioned in scripture, it is always in the context of other sins which most Christians experience. There is never any distinction made about the quality or type of relationship involved. It now seems to me that the only possible way to claim that God does not condemn all sex between same-sex partners, is to say that the scriptures concerned are not God's Word for me today. But to do this would undermine the very foundations of my faith and the truth of the Gospel of Christ.

9

Growing in the Ministry

HAVING SETTLED IN A NEW HOME with my father, the ministry based in my little office (the outhouse!) was still growing, slowly but positively. Following the brief crisis of faith, I now felt more secure, but thought that it would be good to do some more in-depth theological study. I felt this would strengthen my self-confidence, especially when faced by theological students. But how would it be possible? It was suggested to me that I should go away to college for a while. Several friends thought this was a good idea, although I could see many wondering if it would be a step into the ordained ministry. This appealed to a lot of people, I think possibly because it seemed respectable and secure. I would get comments like, 'Martin, I can really see you in a dog collar.' One friend said he wondered if it was really an excuse to get some 'space' away from my father. I think this was one of the reasons the idea of college appealed so much.

Eventually it was decided I should do a Diploma in Theology for two years at Oak Hill College, London. This seemed an obvious choice, mainly because David Field was there, and I felt I could probably keep the ministry 'ticking over' and study at the same time. I applied for a grant but was turned down. 'What was the Lord saying?' I wondered. Then my father offered to pay for the tuition fees, from his life savings. This was yet another example of his amazing generosity. I now felt certain that this was what I wanted to do. If I am honest, I was beginning to feel in something of a rut and rather bored, stale and lonely. The idea of this new experience, away from home and surrounded by lots of students, really appealed. By this time I had tasted quite a lot of student life through my visits to colleges and the friends I made there. My motives for going to Oak Hill were certainly mixed, although I was determined not to see that at the time.

The college is set in lovely wooded grounds, the trees having been planted when the main house was used as a family residence. Having also at one time been partly a small farm, the estate is like a rural oasis in the centre of prosperous north London suburbia. Several buildings had been added to the main house, including a 'New Wing' which is where all the single student accommodation was at that time. Nowadays many new buildings have been added, including even more houses. Many of the married students were housed in the modern housing estate built in the grounds, some of which have been converted from the farm buildings. It was exciting to be shown to my own room. It was obviously purpose built, with highly polished block floors, fitted light oak cupboards and a bookshelf, above which was a very large noticeboard. Although the rooms in the new wing were built in the 1960s, the desks and chairs were a wide variety of shapes and sizes. It was fascinating to see how personal souvenirs, posters and plants transformed these rooms to the individual's personality. One guy even had a complete train set and scenery running around his room. I put the magnificent large, light oak desk which came with the room, in the window overlooking the croquet lawn with squirrels playing in the nearby trees, and the field beyond inhabited by a few cows.

When David Wheaton, the Principal, gave me a verse of scripture in my welcoming interview, I realised its significance to me. It was 2 Timothy 1:14, 'Guard the good deposit that was entrusted to you – guard it with the help of the Holy Spirit who lives in us.' It seemed clear that God was saying that T*f* T must not be neglected. I had the T*f* T mail forwarded to me at college and it was not long before my vision for the ministry was revitalised, largely, I am sure, due to the love and interest from other students.

I learnt so much during my time at college, especially about relationships. Before long, I noticed a slight sense of fear towards me, from many of the students, despite their love, concern and friendliness. We had a rota for meeting together in twos for prayer and some of the men shared this fear, often saying they felt a bit threatened by me. For example, some had been involved in homosexuality at school and had an underlying fear that they might have homosexual leanings. Others were troubled because a homosexual had made a pass at them. Sometimes their response had been one of real anger and they felt guilty about it. With others it seemed that the person making advances to them had thought they were also homosexual, and this left them feeling a bit insecure about their own sexuality. I was able to explain that many homosexuals indulge in wishful thinking that someone they like is also homosexual. These conversations with students opened my eyes to very understandable fears in others that I was hitherto unaware of. It helped me to understand one of the possible reasons for the lack of deep relationships in my own church fellowship.

One of my fellow students, Nigel, was aware of this problem and made a determined effort to get to know me as a person, rather than 'the man with the ministry to homosexuals'. I always found it difficult to make a move towards someone else in terms of friendship because when I made a move there was often no response. Nigel recognised this and made it a goal to get to know me. I am so grateful that he did, as we became very close friends and I valued his deeply loving wisdom and openness very much indeed. It was lovely to have someone to 'drop in on', or go out with, once again. Nigel was a few years younger than me; he was a tall, dark and solidly built man and his quiet, gentle manner and deep desire to understand people made him a person to whom many students turned to share anxieties and frustrations.

Because the ministry continued to grow and develop, it soon became clear that it would not be right to use my father's money for another year at college. I needed to absorb as much of the academic influences as possible, but could not complete the full course adequately and maintain the ministry of T*f*T at the same time. One or the other would have to go – so I left Oak Hill. However, many of the relationships I made there have been kept up, and for me a lot of that 'family feeling' still remains, especially when I return, as I have often done. A few years after I left, David and Margaret Field moved on to pastures new. Amazingly, the current ethics tutor is another young David Field (no relative) and the Principal a keen T*f*T supporter, David Peterson.

During my time at Oak Hill there were some significant developments in the ministry. I was now in contact with similar ministries in the USA. It was encouraging to see how the Lord had led so many of us, independently, down very similar paths of ministry. I was especially glad to have contact with 'Love in Action' (now 'New Hope'), a ministry based in San Rafael (near San Francisco). Some people from 'LIA' moved into the London area during my time at Oak Hill, in the hope of starting a ministry there. This never materialised at that time, but the links established were to prove very significant later.

I also met Elizabeth Moberly, a Christian psychologist, during my time at Oak Hill. Elizabeth was writing a book, following several years of research. She had come to some very positive conclusions about the causes of homosexual development and was attracted to our ministry because of our emphasis, at that time, on meeting same-sex emotional needs. She came to visit me at Oak Hill and we shared our ideas. I was immediately struck by this young woman's personality and tremendous intelligence. A few years earlier I think this would have been very difficult for me to handle, but with some college experience under my belt I no longer felt threatened by academics.

Trying to put it very simply, Elizabeth believes that 'the homosexual condition involves legitimate developmental needs, the fulfilment of which has been blocked by an underlying ambivalence to members of the same sex'. She says that these legitimate same-sex developmental needs have, to various degrees, not been met by the parent of the same sex and have developed into a homosexual desire. She emphasises that the parent should not be held to blame, because the relationship problems could be in the parent, the child or a complex combination of both. It could even have resulted from an early hurt in the child's experience that was not always easy to identify. This usually causes a defensive detachment from the parent of the same sex and a closer attachment to the parent of the opposite sex. This made quite a lot of sense to me, although I was not totally convinced. I can see now that there are a lot of factors involved in this highly complex sexual developmental process – different in each person's experience, as mentioned in the last chapter.

Elizabeth believes the way forward is that the person with homosexual feelings needs to experience affirming, same-sex relationships in adulthood. This should make good the developmental deficit and encourage growth towards heterosexuality. One of the major problems, as I saw it, was in defining the precise quality of these relationships. Deep 'homo-emotional' and erotic feelings will almost certainly be there. Much of the healing will involve working through these feelings to a point of emotional security. A lot of hurts, fears and insecurities from the past would need ministry. 'Inner healing' in many forms, along with other forms of Christian counselling and ministry, would be involved.

TfT had always sought to understand, and where necessary use, whatever form of help the Holy Spirit makes available. It was a challenge to all of us because wholeness and healing always need working through in the everyday situation.

As I learned more about myself and others, I could see the truth in Elizabeth's ideas and it underlined even more the need for greater understanding and experience of relationships in the Body of Christ. The need to be affirmed, wanted and needed (i.e. one's love to be accepted) are very important for us all. I certainly recognised these needs in myself. Right at the start of the ministry I had a letter from one of the Sisters of Mary, which was a word from the Lord for me. She said I needed a mature brother in Christ with whom to share fellowship, to the point of not making any major decision without this brother's knowledge. I knew my heart longed for such a brother. My personal life and ministry seemed dogged by loneliness. Was it really the path the Lord had planned for me? Was I to learn through it total dependence on his love to meet all my needs? I am sure I still needed to experience more of that surrender to Christ, but I also knew that God's love and security were also to be experienced through his people.

I had wondered for a while about the possibility of bringing people who contacted us together, to share Bible study and fellowship. The main purpose in this would be to strengthen and encourage each other, with the hope of experiencing more open relationships within our own fellowships. I obviously had some fears about the possible sexual temptations this kind of group could encourage, but felt they needed to be worked through. It also seemed very important to me that not all members of the group should be from a homosexual background.

The root of problems, experienced by Christians contacting me, were also shared by many people with heterosexual feelings. I found a lot of Christians without experience of homosexuality could identify with my feelings and emotions. There is a tendency to believe that only someone with a homosexual orientation can identify with another homosexual. This is not necessarily true. Two homosexuals may have a same-sex attraction in common, but very little else. Their fears, insecurities, hurts, sexual frustrations and habits may be quite different. On the other hand, a person with heterosexual feelings may well be able to identify in all these areas. Christians (whatever their sexuality) rarely find this out, because they do not seek to relate to someone else on this level. It is often just assumed that the other cannot identify with 'my feelings', because the sexual orientation is not the same.

As mentioned earlier, we called these groups 'Harbinger' groups (since renamed Barnabas) and had our first meeting in London. About seven or eight people turned up on the first Saturday evening – it was a bit tense at first as this kind of meeting was a totally new experience for most of us. The sharing was not on a very deep level, and this proved to be an ongoing problem in the fortnightly Harbinger Groups. However, the time of talking over items for prayer at the end of the meeting seemed the most productive aspect. It provided a time of mutual sharing which happened naturally and usually made the meetings finish late. We decided to cut down the Bible study, which had been intended as a springboard for sharing, to give more time for prayer needs. These meetings continued in London for four years, although latterly they were infrequent, because it was difficult for me to be there. They were later replaced by a new London ministry called Turnabout, which ultimately became T/T in London. Our office in London eventually closed, being replaced by several volunteer Pastoral Support Workers.

During my time at Oak Hill in 1980 the Church of England's Board of Social Responsibility published a very controversial report called 'Homosexual Relationships', which was debated in General Synod (the government of the Church of England). The report was produced by people from a mainly 'liberal' persuasion in terms of biblical authority. It was hardly surprising that they did not come out with a clear 'No' to homosexual relationships. The row within the Church of England was tremendous and Synod would not come to a decision and say where the Church stood on this issue. It was a busy time for T/T, as many churches and church groups were encouraged to look at the subject. We sent a duplicated letter and article to all the members of the Synod, and the students at Oak Hill were a tremendous help in addressing letters. A few of us went to Church House and put them in the members' pigeon holes. We then stayed for the debate. It was very encouraging to hear the late Hugh Silvester (who was on our Council of Reference) mention T/T and myself in a very sensitive and moving speech.

I missed Oak Hill very much, although it was good to feel more invigorated to continue the ministry of T/T. Our contacts and support continued to increase, but they were still mainly men, rather than women.

While I was at Oak Hill, Mike, a minister from Lancashire, began to show interest in our ministry. When I arrived home I met Mike, who shared a lot about a close friend of his, Peter, who was married with two children and another on the way. Mike was very concerned indeed about Peter's homosexual problems. His wife Annette knew about them, and their marriage was in a pretty bad way at that time. I met Mike several times but he seemed unable to persuade Peter to meet me. Then, one day in July 1980 he succeeded. Peter was a fair-haired 25-year-old and obviously nervous. He was a bit reluctant to share at first and so, as usual, I told him a little about myself. He seemed to find it easy to identify with my experiences of relationships and this helped him to talk about his problems with another Christian man, which meant a lot to him. I can remember trying to steer him away from negative feelings. It seemed a very delicate situation and I was nervous of any words or attitude on my part which could possibly cause him to totally reject what I was saying and go right away from his marriage and the Lord. It seems strange, looking back, how our lives have both moved on since that initial meeting. Little did I appreciate the significance of it, as Peter was to become my best friend and eventually to work with me in T*f*T. Many times I would meet people in the course of T*f*T work and wonder if this might be the person the Lord wants as the 'brother in Christ' described by Sister Eulalia and prayed for by so many of our supporters. As usual with God's blessings, in my experience, they come when least expected.

Peter maintained contact with the ministry, as did Mike, and we all became close friends. We decided to form a Harbinger Group in the North West and started fortnightly meetings in my house. As in London, it was difficult to encourage the ten or twelve attending to share very openly. I often felt I had to 'set the pace', which was a bit daunting and challenging.

I was determined to feel less isolated in the ministry and therefore introduced a membership scheme, so that supporters could feel more committed and involved. The idea behind this was for members to contribute ideas, articles and testimonies for our mailing and possibly also have some contact with one another, although that was emphasised less. The other fairly radical change was the introduction of a working party for the ministry. This was made up of Christians who would meet with me regularly, bringing ideas and plans for the future direction of T*f*T. Anything very radical had to be approved by the trustees before being acted upon. The working party would also be able to bring their various gifts to particular areas of the ministry. In future I would be a member of the working party and, it was hoped, not feel so isolated. The trustees happily agreed to this idea, especially as Roy Barker had moved to Cambridge to be Director of Pastoral Studies at Ridley Hall Theological College. This meant that he was not as readily available for instant advice and guidance.

The working party was formed with nine members, although as we progressed, some dropped out and new members were added. The major problem, as far as I was concerned, was they were all at least 40 miles away. However, Peter and Mike were both members and also involved in our North West Harbinger Group, so we did see one another more frequently. They were gradually becoming the 'mainstays' of the team and probably closer to me than anyone else. Peter had been very reluctant to accept my invitation to join at first, though I was convinced that it would be good for him and for us. The sense of purpose and achievement in being used by the Lord would help boost his confidence in himself and God. I had certainly experienced that for myself, even though at times I felt very weak and unworthy. I could identify with the sense of weakness and unworthiness that Peter was experiencing, but could not help him through this barrier.

The Lord had shown me several times, when I was feeling at my weakest and believing I was unable to minister to others, that he wanted to use me at that very time, rather than when I felt strong again. I am not saying this is always God's way, of course. He does not want us to feel continually crippled, but at times our weakness becomes our strength in ministering Christ's love and understanding to others (2 Cor. 12:9–10). There have been times in my ministry when, if I had the choice, I would have avoided counselling situations, because of feeling unworthy. However, the Lord did not give me the chance of 'opting out' and made me aware of how much he wanted my ministry in a specific situation. This was very humbling and made me so aware of God's love that I was greatly blessed and then more determined to obey and follow him. Having said that, I now appreciate the problems which can arise when, rather than being encouraged because we have been used in our weakness, we become even more depressed. This is because Satan, the accuser and deceiver, brings us under condemnation, often calling us hypocrites when we are not. How we need the encouragement and affirmation of God's people! Peter eventually became one of the most valuable members of the working party, although he was probably unaware of it at the time. Through frequent telephone conversations we were able to encourage one another. I know this was true on my part, as he gently nursed me through a few difficult patches. It was good to have a confessor in him.

With the help of the working party we were able to organise our first conference in 1982, called 'Learning to Love', which we held in the Church Hall at Upton. This was a great success – especially in the quality of worship, which we have always seen as a priority for a helpful conference. In this first 'Learning to Love' conference, my friend from college, Nigel, spoke on 'Sexuality and the Single Person' and met his future wife Linda! How wonderful it has been to see them grow together as a married couple. Also a UCCF Travelling Secretary from Manchester, who had previously invited me to speak to a CU, came to this conference and just as we were clearing up at the end, turned to me and said timidly, 'I guess you realise my interest in this subject is more than academic!' He eventually led the T*f*T ministry in London, initially called Turnabout.

The ministries in the USA similar to T*f*T organised themselves into a coalition, called Exodus. There were now also a few ministries in Europe, primarily in Holland, who were similar to us. In fact they had been in existence before we arrived on the scene, although I had not known about them. Our friends in Holland organised a conference which they called 'Exodus International – Europe' and a few of us from the working party, including Peter and his wife Annette, went along. Geoffrey Percival, from Pilot, also joined us. This was quite a breakthrough in terms of Annette's involvement in the ministry. The Lord exposed many of her understandable insecurities and brought healing and a sense of feeling able to be a part of this ministry.

I had been talking and sharing a lot about relationships and the way in which God can meet many of our needs through them, but I was conscious of not really living the kind of lifestyle I was encouraging as part of the healing process. Then a young student came to see me. He had been told to come by his tutor at Bible College, as a condition for his remaining there. He was obviously hurting and said he had been through general counselling, 'deliverance' and 'inner healing' sessions. None of them seemed to have worked and he was very disillusioned with evangelicalism. As he talked, it became very evident that he was crying out for love, so I shared with him the road, in terms of Christian love and affection, I believed God wanted him to travel. Then my safe and secure position as a counsellor was shattered as he said, 'Well, as you've been saying all this about what I should be experiencing, is it possible for you to show me some love and affection?' 'Help!' I thought, 'How on earth do I respond? If I say 'No' to him, he will just dismiss all that I have said and accuse me of the same hypocrisy as some of the other evangelicals he knows. On the other hand . . . is what he is suggesting professional?' I was confused, but felt at least I must try to offer him something different, otherwise he was quite likely in his present frame of mind to join the 'gay church'. So I nervously took the plunge and entered into a close friendship with this man. Needless to say, all this was totally unprofessional conduct on my part. The friendship was certainly not right in the way it developed, despite the fact that I insisted on total honesty about any sexual arousal either of us might feel, in order to prevent our relationship travelling in the wrong direction.

After my initial hesitation the relationship deepened and I found that I was being helped and comforted by this friend's tender affection. I had not experienced anything like this for a number of years, and found that the love and affirmation I received took the lid off my emotions. We became very affectionate and emotionally involved with one another. I must have grieved the Lord in many ways, although we just about managed to prevent sex taking place. I remember him joining one of our group meetings and to my horror announcing, 'You need to know my relationship with Martin is not orgasmic!'

Eventually my friend ended our relationship, having become aware, as I think I was, that it could not continue in the direction in which it was going. We were both hurt, but had the friendship continued it would have meant the end of my involvement with T*f*T, not to mention a right relationship with God. This episode did, however, serve to reveal needs in me – needs for love, affection and commitment – which were much stronger than I had imagined. Was this really what Elizabeth Moberly was talking about? How did

God want to meet these deep-rooted needs, some of which had been freshly exposed? The support of Peter and other members of the working party at this time was invaluable. The complex and difficult area of deeply committed Christian relationships was being opened up to us. How were our theories, if they were right, going to be put into practice? After eight years as a Christian, I thought I knew quite a lot about relationships in the Lord, but in fact I was only beginning to scratch the surface.

As the Lord increased the number of men and women prepared to help in the ministry, so people contacted us with problems which only our new helpers could really understand. For example, more women were now in touch with us, and not surprisingly their experiences were often very different from the men. We also met married women unaware of any homosexual feelings until their thirties or forties. A typical situation would be one in which a married woman developed a close relationship with another female. She would suddenly become aware of strong sexual and emotional feelings towards this woman and would be horrified to think she might be 'homosexual'. Women with homosexual feelings seem to be especially prone to very strong emotional dependency, although of course it also happens with men if they allow it to. It is so often a question of agonising the situation through before God, knowing that a relationship which usurps our dependence on him is very risky for Christians. A degree of dependence in terms of security and commitment is necessary, but we have to be on our guard against idolatry and, of course, possible sexual involvement. That is why we need someone uninvolved with the situation, a committed Christian, who can help us to live in the light and bring our feelings and actions to God. This person needs to know all that is happening.

Several of our contacts were considering marriage and this was an area in which Peter and Annette were able to counsel and advise. We already knew of a few men who married, thinking it would solve all their homosexual problems. The result was often a disastrous marriage relationship. On the other hand however, once people from a homosexual background were finding the temptations decreasing, and sometimes even ceasing, relationships with Christian women were developing. This would start as a friendship in which both people were very honest about their feelings and problems. An emotional bond would develop and sometimes an awareness of sexual feelings for each other. In marriages which develop from this beginning, it seems the husband with homosexual feelings is aware of a sexual desire for his wife, but often not for other women, although there is usually still a potential for homosexual problems to exist. We can always hold out the possibility of marriage for someone from a homosexual background, but it must be entered into very carefully and prayerfully. Never should marriage be considered as the answer for homosexual difficulties. In fact, heterosexual relations in marriage can actually bring homosexual feelings to the surface all the more. Sadly, Christians with homosexual feelings often, but not always, long for marriage because it will make them 'feel more normal'. I believe this is one of Satan's deceptions.

We are sometimes asked about the satanic influences in homosexuality. I often imagine people envisage hundreds of gay demons floating around, like something from *The Rocky Horror Show*! In my experience the major attacks of Satan in homosexuality are centred around accusation and deception, usually thriving on secrecy and fear. One of the best ways to stop the enemy capitalising on secrecy is to 'live in the light' with another brother or sister in Christ. This should be someone who knows and loves us. We must be aware that what we have to share will sometimes hurt that loved one, especially if it involves sin or even temptation. This gives us an incentive to avoid difficult situations and refrain from playing with temptation because we know it will have to be shared with someone we love. In a sense, I believe accountability should mean the person is 'with us' in the area of potential temptation, which often takes the power of it away. I was soon to find this tremendously valuable in my relationship with Peter (James 5:16).

In 1982 my brother died suddenly from a heart attack, while watching television. Most of my father's friends said it was 'a happy release for him'. Certainly his life over the last decade had been one of a recluse, rarely leaving his flat. His problems had caused a tremendous financial and emotional drain on my parents. He almost seemed to want to destroy all his friendships. I felt sad that, at his funeral, only two of his close friends who were there said they would miss him. He had, however, taught us all a lot, despite his difficulties.

10
Vision of a Family

───◄o►───

EARLY IN MY CHRISTIAN EXPERIENCE I was aware of some of the problems facing single people in the Church. One way through this, I thought, could be a development of the idea of Christian community, although I actually felt the traditional idea of Christian community discouraged individuality. I wondered if it would be possible for people to live together in a large house, each with their own bed-sitting room, but meeting together in communal rooms. In this way the individual could express his or her personality and even entertain to some extent in their own room. However they would also eat, relax and entertain with other members of the household. I guess I saw it as the 'best of both worlds' – community and fellowship plus independence.

As the ministry developed, the importance of the right sort of Christian relationships was apparent, both through my own experiences and those of people contacting us. I knew the sort of relationship for which I longed, and believed it to be honouring to the Lord, albeit probably a bit risky. Although I felt I could cope with more than one close relationship (I acknowledged that very many would be impossible to handle emotionally), there did not seem to be anyone in my own life fulfilling what I considered a legitimate need at this time.

When Peter was a teenager and struggling with his homosexual problems, he cried to the Lord one night and God told him that some day he would be helping people with similar problems to his own. Since becoming more involved with T*f*T Peter had wondered several times if he should take on more of a role in the ministry. At one stage I thought about the possibility of opening a coffee shop, with Peter, Annette and myself working together and also with T*f*T. Peter was unemployed at the time but the door to this plan was quite firmly closed. The overheads involved made it impractical. Then Peter managed to get a job and soon started buying a house. However, the possibility of a return to full-time Christian work was always with him. He knew the job he had with a petrol station company would not last for ever and it seemed that when eventually it did come to an end, this would be the time to think again about Christian work.

Peter and I had encouraged and ministered to one another as we both tasted something of Christian relationships. We were both looking for a person or people who would meet the same-sex emotional needs that Elizabeth Moberly felt were so important. In the closeness that was beginning to develop between Peter, myself and increasingly, Annette, we mentioned the idea of community from time to time, but only semi-seriously. Peter had always been impressed by some Christians he knew in Eastbourne who lived together as a large family and shared the love of Christ from their home to many people. At Christmas 1982, Peter, Annette and the children stayed at my house over the New Year. They had been keen to cancel the whole idea, wondering how on earth they would cope with the children and my father in such a close atmosphere. Much to our amazement, it was quite a success. Again, only half seriously, we wondered if this was a foretaste of community living!

The time came when some positive steps had to be taken. Peter's job was soon to end and Philip, his eldest son, was due to move schools, in September 1983. Peter and Annette did not want him to start at this school and then be uprooted. We prayed about it and I talked over the idea with my father. He was amazing, and said he would fall in with our plans and did not want to stand in the way. We all felt it would help bring a new dimension to his life and hopefully end some of the loneliness he was experiencing. Where would we live? There seemed to be nothing in Rochdale, where they were living, but I found a few possible houses in the Birkenhead area. If we were to live together it looked as if it would be in Birkenhead. At Eastertime we decided to 'lay a fleece' before the Lord, so that if it was right there would be a buyer for our house by June 1983.

Both Peter and I knew that one of our reasons for living together like this would be to help meet our emotional needs and in doing that provide an environment of love in the home and between us all, which visitors could see and experience for themselves. Hence the answers we believed God had for the person with homosexual problems would be seen in action, rather than simply in theory.

I had been asked to be President of 'Exodus International –

Europe', and was given the job of organising the May 1983 conference. We chose Ashburnham Place in Sussex and thought we would try to get Jim Bigelow from the USA as our main speaker, with 'Loving Relationships in the Body of Christ' as our theme. Jim had written an excellent book called *Love Has Come Again*, but I doubted that he would be available for our conference. Contacting him was really a 'shot in the dark', so I was thrilled when he accepted. We also invited Elizabeth Moberly to speak on homosexuality and transsexuality.

The conference was a success and I found Jim's talks especially encouraging. I was able to share with him a little of my own experiences, ideas and hopes as well as fears. He encouraged me a lot. I still had some reservations about relating on a deep emotional level to a married man like Peter. In some ways, the future still seemed almost unreal because no positive moves and decisions had yet been made. However, there was a growing bond of love between us.

When June arrived we had two potential buyers for the house and both could complete the transaction. We felt the Lord was saying that we should proceed with caution. By this time, Peter had been made redundant and Annette took on a job as manager for a household container firm. This provided a car as well as some additional income. Peter was able to come over to Birkenhead for the day occasionally to help out with office work. Our relationship started to develop and there was a sense of commitment for the future. He was showing me love and affection that meant a lot. I knew there was no sexual attraction there on his side and at that time I wasn't aware of particularly strong feelings in that direction either. I remember one incident when Peter and the family were going away to France for a holiday, provided by someone we met at Ashburnham. Before they left Peter said, 'It doesn't seem fair, somehow, I feel you should be coming as well.' It meant a lot to know of this newly found love and commitment to me.

The sale of our house was fraught with problems. There was always a potential buyer, but then at the last minute it would fall through, and it sometimes seemed as if the Lord was opening a door for us and then shutting it. Despite all this, we still believed that God was saying 'Go ahead', because the situation on the house sale never completely fell through. Whenever we questioned whether our plans were right with God, something would happen

Vision of a Family

which encouraged us to continue. Eventually it became clear that a positive decision regarding the move would have to be taken because of Philip's schooling. He would have to be transferred to Birkenhead by September 1983 and so Peter and Annette decided to move Philip over to his new school. He would stay in our house with Peter, myself and my father, and Annette and the other children would stay in their house in Rochdale until it was sold and our new home together was found. This was to be longer than we anticipated, but there is no doubt it was a part of God's plan, because it served several purposes. Although it was a difficult time of separation for Peter and Annette, it strengthened their marriage relationship. It also brought a new closeness to Peter and Philip's relationship. This important time helped my father, Peter and Philip to get to know one another and, of course, Peter and I had to work at our relationship together in this new situation. God had been good to us, because many of the additional pressures of home and family life for Peter and Philip were taken away. There were, of course, problems – Peter and his family obviously missed one another during the week. This situation was to continue for about six months, until May 1984.

Now I was beginning to find how little I really did know about loving – I'm sure the mistakes I made would fill another book! It was as if all my 'insecurity buttons' were being pressed, one by one. Some of them were surfacing through my sexuality. It was certainly good that Peter wasn't sexually attracted to me because I was even questioning how I could be loved, if I wasn't desired sexually. When I reluctantly admitted this to myself, it came as a shock. Peter must have been really struggling to love through all this, but we were still convinced, most of the time, we were following God's plan for us.

It seemed some foundations for the future were clearly being laid by the Lord and he showed us that the first step must be one of commitment, to God and to one another. Jim Bigelow had showed us that when God said, 'It is not good for the man to be alone' (Gen. 2:18) it was while God and man still had a perfect relationship, unmarred by sin. Therefore even before the Fall, God was saying, 'I have created you to need someone else apart from me.' So we do need someone else apart from God. This legitimate human need for another person, or people, had been a major emotional driving force in my life for many years. Now, as a Christian, I was able to see God encouraging and empowering this need in me. It all seemed very appealing. Of course I would have said my relationship with God was the most important one. However, it wasn't until many years later that I realised how much I was really using human relationships as an attempt to find emotional security and self-worth. I read that we need to learn to be alone with ourselves and God in order to properly relate to others, but didn't really understand what that meant.

Jim Bigelow showed us how many of the relationships we see in scripture involved a deep commitment. For example, 'Jonathan made a covenant with the house of David . . . And Jonathan had David reaffirm his oath out of love for him, because he loved him as he loved himself' (1 Samuel 20:16–17). It was the same for the friendship between Ruth and Naomi: 'Ruth replied, "Don't urge me to leave you or to turn back from you. Where you go I will go, and where you stay I will stay. Your people will be my people and your God my God. Where you die I will die, and there I will be buried. May the LORD deal with me, be it ever so severely, if anything but death separates you and me"' (Ruth 1:16–17).

It may not always be right to make that sort of commitment, but something akin to it is important in a relationship of great depth. It is obviously not possible to relate to a lot of people like that. It seems from the Gospels that Jesus was especially close to just three disciples, Peter, James and John.

It gave me a great sense of personal joy and security to affirm an oath of love for Peter and Annette and to be able to substantiate that by means of a will and eventually joint house ownership. A friendship often needs a solid commitment before the Lord, to hold it together, when everything around and often the people themselves are being torn apart. It was certainly to prove true in our lives.

It was not long before we all discovered many of our fears and insecurities. As soon as I could see I was causing Peter to feel a bit threatened by my leadership in T*f*T, I made a conscious effort to make him feel in the same place as myself, in terms of authority in the ministry. This was a mistake in many ways because Peter actually needed to feel less pressure of responsibility. I should have taken more of a positive lead, both at work and in our relationship, because Peter was constantly battling with his reactions to my indecision and lack of organisation. I developed a very deep love for him, and with that, many insecurities and fears, usually related to past incidents in my life, surfaced. I often demanded more than he could give. I was beginning to make Peter feel smothered and what started as a very open relationship, in terms of sharing problems and difficulties, became far less so. I often became suspicious and hurt, which in turn hurt Peter. I was also aware of stronger sexual feelings for him than were there at the beginning. Although I knew in theory that his love for me should not depend on any sexual attractiveness, I often found it difficult to believe that I was wanted and I therefore sought affirmation from him. I clearly remember (with a smile now but not at the time) one occasion when I said to Peter, 'You don't really want a relationship with me, do you?' He replied, 'Martin it's not what I want but what God wants that matters!' This was not what I honestly wanted to hear!

I guess there was an ambivalence because I knew that any sexual involvement or even interest (if it were mutual) would cause a big threat to his marriage and probably mean the end of our 'community'. That was one reason I did not want him to find me attractive. Yet I found it difficult to believe I was loved without that. The Lord had a lot of work to do with both of us, but there were many positive areas of healing as well, during our time together. We learned a lot, even though sometimes it seemed like two steps forward and two or even three steps back. I also found a strong love developing for Annette, as we were beginning to relate together as a 'family'.

It was wonderful to experience a partnership in the ministry. Despite all the problems, in the good times it was great to know I was loved and I experienced this assurance through Peter's commitment and also in gentle signs of affection and affirmation. He learnt to know when I was hurting without my saying a word, and I could sense when he was under pressure or perhaps feeling threatened by a person or situation. I had not really experienced quite this depth of love before as a Christian, although my relationships with Tim and John had been very special indeed. I guess beginning to live together was giving these relationships a whole new dimension of truth and honesty that I'd not known to this extent before.

We were, however, especially aware of the enemy's hand bringing division and misunderstanding. This was usually related to a significant time, like a meeting or project we were undertaking. But on many occasions we also saw the Lord bring a tremendous reconciliation and healing. If we were going to grow

Still Learning to Love

in Christ, we needed to understand more of him and more of one another.

Suddenly, the house situation changed dramatically. Peter and Annette's house was sold and they had to be out by May. At last it looked as if we had a sale going through on my house as well, but we had not yet found our large 'family home'. The Lord seemed to be saying to us it would all be an 'eleventh hour' situation, which would work out in the end. We contacted local housing associations to see if there was any chance of temporary accommodation for Peter and Annette, but they held out no hope. Then, a little over a week before they were due to move out of their home, the housing association came up with an excellent four-bedroomed terraced house for rent, which was amazingly cheap and could be used as a temporary measure.

Then we saw an eight-bedroom Victorian house in Birkenhead which seemed ideal for us as a family. It needed a lot of work and was therefore possibly within our price range. It had been originally on the market for £79,000 but most of the fittings had since been removed. We felt it right to offer £31,000 and to our surprise they accepted. Father and I now had a sale going through on our own house with a 'first-time buyer' (very unusual for this type of property). The Lord certainly had moved at the 'eleventh hour'! Peter, with a lot of help from Mike, worked on the renovations and eventually, in July 1984, father and I moved into a couple of the upstairs rooms as a temporary measure. The renovations included fitting all new bathrooms and toilets, as well as rewiring and extensive plumbing – a major undertaking for Peter who was in charge of the operation and did all the major work. He said once, from under the floorboards, that he was gripped with fear at the prospect of all the work and responsibility he had to face. But he then remembered an old hymn, 'Because He lives, I can face tomorrow' and he started singing it in the gloom and dust.

When Peter and Annette eventually moved in there were still misunderstandings and frictions, although most of the fears we had beforehand were not realised. The major problem was a lack of understanding, as we tended to have preconceived ideas about the way each other would react in a given situation. Our mutual love and acceptance were still growing. The careless comments and misunderstandings became fewer. I was proud of my new family and learning to love Peter, Annette and the children in a very special way.

11
The Family – Hurting and Healing

A VERY DAUNTING AND COMPLETELY DIFFERENT lifestyle was now beginning. Not as dramatically different as joining a community or becoming a monk, but traumatic, to say the least. I had made one of the most important decisions of my life. Was it going to work? So many Christians had written about their lives in 'extended families' and communities, often with enough negatives to put us off the idea. I am not too keen on phrases such as 'extended family' or 'community'. They sound almost clinical to me. I prefer to simply use the word 'family'. We are closely related through our parents and grandparents, but surely the blood of Jesus and the Holy Spirit within each of us is a much closer family bond than any other? My family are my family through Jesus and our mutual commitment. Peter kept comparing our relationships with that of a newly married couple. It may sound a strange comparison to some, but how right he was in lots of ways.

We all moved into our large new home together with different anxieties. We sometimes convinced ourselves that problems should be there, when in fact they were not. For example, our tastes in furnishing were not all that dissimilar, when we imagined they would be poles apart. Had this not been the case, however, I was aware that my timidity could have made me accept what I did not like, and I sometimes did, for the sake of not causing any problems – a terrible reflection on my own weakness and vulnerability. In many ways I was reliving my relationships with friends in childhood. The same 'tape' was playing in my subconscious – 'I will learn to do whatever you do in order that you will accept me.' In childhood this was playing football and cricket with my friends, now it was a much more difficult 'game' and I felt something like a loser from the start. Nevertheless, we all kept reminding ourselves that the Lord had brought all this about for a purpose and we must trust him.

Although we emphasised that the house was to be a family home, not a centre for T*f*T or a 'community' home, we decided to have a housewarming/dedication. We organised this and 80 people attended.

The house provided us with a living room and kitchen each; a dining room and what had been a games room. This room was panelled with wood, possibly from a Victorian church or chapel. Because there were no windows on the wall, but simply skylights, we saw it as excellent for 'ministry' and meetings. There was plenty of light from the 'peaked' roof, but also some water leaks and a lot of cold air! When we had enough money, we decided, it would be insulated and carpeted properly. At the dedication we managed to squeeze the 80 people into that room, and hear Roy Barker share God's Word for us. In his lovely way, he gave us three letters – 'OAP'. We must be 'Open' to God and one another. We would experience 'Affliction'. We must 'Persevere'. Those words have certainly proved prophetic! We sent teams of people around the house to pray in every room. We heard interesting reports on some of the prayers in the kitchens and bedrooms, especially Peter and Annette's bedroom! I assume they were not too concerned about mine?

There was still a lot of remedial work and alterations to be done on the house, although the main living rooms were finished. Peter was well qualified for this type of work as an electrician and plumber (his father's trade). It was a tremendous challenge for him to take on the renovation, which meant re-fitting the sinks, baths and lavatories (all of which had been removed) and adding new ones also. Mike rewired the house with him, to a very high standard. Peter had been released from T*f*T's ministry to work on the house for six months prior to the dedication. Often working on his own, it became a heavy burden. Although one of our local supporters had very generously paid for an unemployed man to help with the redecoration, there were still tremendous pressures on Peter. I personally lacked a lot of self-confidence in the practical area, because of Peter's professionalism. In the past I had undertaken some work on houses I owned, but, in this situation, I was very conscious of my efforts not coming up to Peter's high standards. I was able to do some wall-scraping and even a little decorating, but felt very much like a nervous child seeking to please his parent. This was ironic considering Peter was twelve years younger than me. The last thing he needed at this stage was yet another child!

Although there was still some work to be done on our home, we eventually felt it should be 'shelved', to give Peter a break and bring him back into the ministry of T*f*T.

T*f*T's ministry was still growing during this period, but now took on a very exciting new dimension. This seemed to coincide with the publication of an article about Peter and Annette in *Family* magazine. Married couples were coming to Peter and Annette for counselling, the majority of cases being where the husband had homosexual problems. Some people contacted us as a result of the article, or simply through hearing about T*f*T's ministry in some other way. It was a great encouragement to see the Lord developing Peter and Annette's ministry and giving them more confidence, in very much the same way as he had for me. If he had once felt daunted by people like academics, clergy and doctors, the Lord dealt with it by bringing them to us for help! The threat disappears when you discover that they are vulnerable and hurting too. It was certainly true for me and I assumed for Peter and Annette, although I'm not sure that was really the case. People started to come and stay at our home for a few days and the Lord ministered to them in wonderful ways. This was often when we, either individually or corporately, felt very weak and unworthy – how gracious God is!

The Lord was teaching us all a lot about ourselves and, as we were ministered to by others, our own ministry developed. Needless to say, before long we all became too busy. While this was not so much of a problem for me as an individual, it laid a great deal of pressure on Peter and his family. It was difficult to escape from T*f*T. Annette and the children needed Peter's time, and then there was the running of the house with so many practical jobs which needed doing. If we relaxed and did nothing we had to force ourselves not to feel guilty, especially if one of the others was busy. We decided that more structure was needed in terms of a timetable. At that stage we spent little, if any time, relaxing together and, even worse, we seldom prayed together except in a crisis. Perhaps we were seeking the impossible – living separately, yet together.

When my mind wasn't focused on the ministry, it was often in a state of emotional turmoil. I wanted to be a better friend to Peter and meet more of his needs. I tried, rather pathetically, to prove that I could do this and usually failed dismally. The more I thought

I had let go, the more Peter got the opposite impression. He sensed, quite naturally, how much he was on my mind and therefore the pressure of feeling smothered was there as much as ever. I was encouraged to develop other interests and relationships. I lacked a lot of enthusiasm for this. As a Christian, I felt I had tried in the past to make close friendships and it only worked a few times. Was this my fault? I think not entirely, but I could have persevered much more than I did.

I was on a self-defeating downwards spiral. The more I failed in my relationship with Peter and others in the house, the weaker and more insecure I felt. This caused even more pressure, especially on Peter, who felt guilty, hurt and even angry that he could not respond in the way I was demanding. I knew I was loved by Peter and Annette. It seemed ungrateful of me to want to be *needed* as well. How could they be expected to need someone who so often made them feel guilty and seemed not to appreciate the love that was already there? It often took a crisis situation to bring us to the point of sharing our feelings together and this was usually, but not always, with the help of a Christian friend, Walter. Quite often Annette and I were able to share together, but this was not always right when Peter might become the topic of our conversation. Nevertheless, there were some very positive developments in my relationship with Annette, and a lot of the awkwardness, which I had often felt with women, was broken down.

I began to understand that being able to consider myself part of such a family, even as an 'adopted child', was helping me more than I realised. I was also learning to love the children very much (or perhaps I should say, the 'other children'). There were times when I was left to look after them for a few days. Sometimes I reached screaming pitch, as their parents did at times. They were clearly better at parenting than I was! However, experiencing the children's love, and feeling our relationships develop, was very beautiful for me.

Needless to say, my insecurities came flooding to the surface once again when Peter met a Christian man with whom he could identify and respect. They became very close friends. Paul lived two-and-a-half hours away by car and came to stay for a couple of days and then almost once a week. He was a very nice person, but I felt deeply threatened and hurt. It seemed as if I was being rejected, although of course I was not. I kept trying to convince myself that if

I was really loving in the right way I should be pleased for Peter. But that just seemed to increase the guilt. That was how I should have felt, but I was not there yet. Sometimes, if allowed, my insecurity erupted as anger, 'It's not fair, after my struggles – living and working with someone – another person gets all the candy when I have to suffer the nitty-gritty everyday difficulties.' Quite naturally, my reaction pushed Peter even further away, although he so often tried to help me. Life frequently felt like a nightmare. If only I could escape, run away, as from boarding school, then I could cope – but facing the hurt almost every day often became unbearable. Paul seemed to be all the things I wished I could be. He was experienced in house building and joinery. He played squash and other sports that Peter was beginning to enjoy. He would visit for an evening and they would go out for a drink together. It was made very clear that 'two's company, three's a crowd'. Annette understandably felt annoyed that I should be jealous, when she was prepared to accept Peter's new relationship. There were strict boundaries of course in terms of the time they spent together and there were certainly no sexual feelings involved as far as Peter was concerned.

If I was finding living together difficult, then this was also true for Peter and Annette. Yet we could not escape. Learning to love is not about escaping from problems. The Lord was allowing this for a reason, but the enemy, Satan, was also very active. He would capitalise on our vulnerabilities, especially when we were about to embark on some ministry for the Lord. The attacks often seemed unbearable, but Christ was always victorious, although we usually didn't experience this until the last minute. For example, before a speaking engagement I would be feeling depressed. I asked myself, 'How can I possibly speak to these people?' The Lord always undertook in even the seemingly impossible situations.

But there were some very positive times amidst all the doom and gloom. For example, Peter and I were learning to minister together effectively. The Lord was beginning to heal a lot of the self-consciousness about this that arose from my fears and insecurities which had spoilt our relationship and destroyed a lot of Peter's respect for me in the past. While on a visit to All Nations College we gave the students the opportunity to speak to either one of us, or both. They all chose to see us together and one student actually wanted the two of us to pray with him. Through this we were shown the need to release one another's ministry to the Lord. It was actually the Holy Spirit's ministry, not ours, and we had to appreciate that and not question what the other might or might not be doing. With that kind of confidence in the Lord and self-discipline, there was much more unity between us – disunity had so often been caused by focusing too much on the problems in our relationship and not enough on God. I think the Lord was showing us that the fundamental problem was the same in both of us, namely a lack of self-acceptance. This is a major problem for so many Christians, of course, and is manifested in a multitude of ways, some more obvious than others. Guilt also plays a vital part, especially in the perfectionist, who cannot accept himself or herself because of unrealistic demands and expectations.

One of the ways a lack of self-acceptance comes to the surface is when someone only feels really secure with another person who appears to be just like themselves, or the way they would like to be. In my case I saw in Peter something of the qualities I would have liked. On the other hand, Peter often saw in me quite a lot of what he believed to be his own weaknesses. When this happens there is likely to be a clash in a relationship. It was therefore often the underlying lack of self-acceptance in both of us which caused a problem. So what is the point in all this hurting of one another, the mixture of love, hurt, anger and bitterness? It seemed, when we moved to our new home together after the months of waiting, there was a lot of rebuilding work to be done in our relationships. Yet, through all this we experienced some healing in ourselves and in one another. When the masks were off, we were vulnerable; but God is not about demolishing, without rebuilding. I was constantly reminded by the Lord that I made a covenant before him in terms of a commitment to Peter and Annette. Scripture shows that such commitments are not to be taken lightly, and certainly not to be broken. For example, David honoured his commitment to Jonathan, even after his death. When the Gibeonites asked for the lives of seven of Saul's descendants, David spared Jonathan's son, 'because of the oath before the Lord between David and Jonathan' (2 Samuel 21:7). Psalm 15 reminds us how important openness and honesty are in relationships as part of our commitment. The Lord honours the man 'who keeps his oath even when it hurts' (Psalm 15:4).

I was very conscious of the ways in which Peter and Annette were seeking to help me. Our openness was developing, although I was still a bit reluctant. I was able to share difficulties (not concerning Peter) with Annette and she made it clear to me that she understood and was sensitive to my feelings. Peter and Annette were very good at being honest with other Christians and seeking reconciliation in relationships. I tended to avoid any possible confrontation and to hide, but thankfully they wouldn't let me get away with it. We also felt it important to involve my father more in these situations. He had obviously realised I was depressed and anxious at times. Sharing even a few of my feelings with him was something of a breakthrough in our relationship. God was certainly doing something with all of us, but it was often difficult to see clearly and identify.

12
Taking a Journey

'THE LORD GAVE ME A PICTURE of your house and it seemed to be in flames. It was under attack from outside.' The woman who shared this with us had never seen the house before, but it became clear that her vision was an accurate one. Some of the details she described could not have been revealed to her by anyone. We accordingly shared something of our problems with this friend, and she felt we needed to have a group of people supporting us both practically and spiritually. She also pointed out the importance of worship within the house – this made sense to me as my own feelings of love and security with the Lord have frequently been rekindled in the atmosphere of worship and adoration. Our monthly 'Praise Meeting', which we held on a Saturday evening, was developing into a regular group of about twenty. At first we used a lot of lively choruses and sought to encourage lively worship, but the atmosphere was beginning to change. As people started to feel relaxed and at home with one another, there was a little more informality and sharing. The worship tended to be gentle and subdued.

Many of the Christian counsellors we met had shared their own experience within a group therapy-type support team. Counsellors need ongoing counsel and healing too! If you hadn't realised that before, you can see how true it is in my case. Perhaps these worship meetings would give birth in some way to our much-needed support?

I had come a long way, in terms of learning to love God, others and myself. In fact we had all come a long way in these areas, although it seemed there was often one of us in a state of hopelessness, when the others were feeling more positive. And yet, whatever our feelings, the Holy Spirit led us into deeper areas of counselling for others. We were all being used by God, and many people said they were greatly helped by our ministry. However, I still fell prey to another attack of depression, this time a really bad one. 'What's the point Lord? . . . We aren't meeting one another's needs . . . Please help me . . . I can't cope any more. Take me home!' My world seemed frightening and hostile but I could not run away. I realised these feelings were not really justified and I was being very ungrateful for all the love I had been given – but I couldn't seem to stop these negative feelings.

God's ways are indeed wonderful and strange. In all this gloom, there was a spark of encouragement. Tim, the person used in my conversion, had played little part in my life of late. We kept in touch, but I knew as little of what was happening in his life as he knew of mine. We began meeting together again, and he soon realised how vulnerable and depressed I was. It happened that he was also going through a traumatic emotional crisis. We talked, prayed and wept together in a way we had never done before. Weeping was becoming increasingly easier for me, which must have indicated some positive healing in that area. It seemed, after fourteen years, that Tim and I were actually getting to know one another, to some extent on a more honest level than before.

A few months earlier, Peter had been to a Christian Gestalt conference. Gestalt, literally translated, means 'wholeness'. The term is more widely used to describe a number of counselling techniques used to discover the path towards wholeness. It involves facing up to or confronting a feeling or experience by, in a sense, re-experiencing it in the here and now. That's probably an inaccurate description of Gestalt, but the best I can do in a few words and limited experience. Like other areas of secular counselling, the Lord often uses it with remarkable results. There can clearly be dangers in some secular techniques, but many of them employ principles of forgiveness, reconciliation and a valuing of oneself that we can experience through God. In other words, they can become a catalyst to finding God's truth, which sets us free.

Peter was helped by the Christian-based Gestalt course. Sadly, although we had hoped to continue the work started with the leader, Ian Davidson, this did not turn out to be practical. One of our supporters suggested that I should book in for the next 'Gestalt Week', which I did. At this Gestalt Conference and at another conference in France, which I attended immediately prior to it, I experienced the type of ministry where one is encouraged to relax and take an imaginary journey. At one stage we were asked to imagine being in a beautiful, secluded part of the countryside and later drew a picture we had seen on this trip. My sense of hopelessness was very evident in the confusion I pictured around a symbol of the Cross. On another occasion we were taken on an imaginary journey down a busy main road and then off into a side street, where we saw an empty shop with just one object in it, a spinning wheel. It was a bit dusty, but very valuable. Why had it been left there? It had been abandoned by mistake. The owners had done a 'moonlight flit'. I was asked to become that object. The journey continued back to the busy main street and to a hypermarket where I could buy anything I wanted. I decided to buy something that would make me into a beautiful acceptable person. That seemed unrealistic so I chose a convertible car, and was asked to become that object. As with the car, I was not as beautiful and perfect as I had at first thought. In fact on close examination I actually had a few spots of rust!

For many of us – certainly for me – these journeys were very revealing. I asked for help (termed 'bidding to work') from my group of eight people. Some simple prayers were offered to the Lord and I was asked to repent of sins, including a hidden one of deception. I 'let go' and fell onto a mattress on the floor. I can't actually remember landing on it – it seemed as if I was floating and I was filled with a tremendous sense of love for the Lord and a feeling of security. There was no embarrassment at all. The only physical sensation was a tingling throughout my body. It seemed almost like a 'spiritual blood transfusion', flowing through me. As I lay there I was encouraged by the leader to 'speak' to Peter and Annette, even though they were not present. 'Use your new blood confidently, to speak to Peter', he coaxed. My words seemed to flow quite naturally, without any premeditation. I affirmed my love for Peter and Annette, expressing my feelings of security and acknowledging that I had a lot to give them. 'I am not your hurting child any more . . . I am a man. I am going to stand on that authority.' I also expressed my sorrow for the ways in which I had caused hurt. As I lay there the words seemed to be coming spontaneously from my heart, rather than from my mind. In some ways it was as if I was not really in control and yet I knew it was really me. The best way of describing it seemed to be as a response to the leader's direction – it was the result of my 'spiritual blood transfusion'. Another member of the group wrote down ('scripted') all that I said. I must

Taking a Journey

admit the – 'I am a man' – bit made me smile much later when I read my script again!

The experience had a marked effect. From then on I knew I did not have to please in order to gain love and acceptance. I was fairly confident in my new-found security, but rather like a bird learning to fly, still felt a little uncertain about what had actually happened and how it would affect my life and relationships.

I travelled to Hayward's Heath to attend a retreat and was joined there by Peter and Annette. How would I respond to them? How would they respond to me? There were only nine of us on the retreat, including the two leaders. It was wonderfully friendly and informal. Then we were asked if we would like to go on an imaginary journey! 'Another one!' I thought, 'Lord, what is this all about? What are you trying to do?'

This time we were asked to walk on a lonely but moonlit path up a mountain. I took a path on the right towards a cave, where an old man greeted me. I sensed a tremendous cleanliness and purity about him, both physically and spiritually. He had immeasurable wisdom. I was told to share with him an important question on my mind, concerning the future implications of what I had experienced over the past couple of weeks. The old man gave me assurance and confidence for the future. It was going to be all right. Then I was told he would give me something. He reached into his cloth bag and put a beautiful glass egg in my hand. It was very smooth and as clear as crystal, yet it glistened with a multitude of colours reflected within. Every time I looked at it, there was something different and more beautiful to be seen. I sensed that the man had given it as a token of all that he shared with me. Yet it was more than that, it almost seemed like a kind of sacrament. Then, to my surprise, I was told to become this object! Wow! – I did and it seemed to seal within me the hope the wise old man had shared. I became myself again and left to go back down the mountain with my precious egg. Just before I left the mountain path I was asked to look again at my gift and see something unnoticed before. I looked into the beautiful glass object and saw . . . myself! I was stunned. It was totally unexpected. In fact I cannot remember any more of the journey, the revelation had such an impact on me.

On reflection it seemed clear that God had used these journeys to affirm within me all that had been happening over these two weeks. I was a valuable person of immense worth to God. My relationships with others could be secure on that foundation. I had known that in theory of course, but the Lord in his wonderful way had transformed it into a vivid experience. A memory and experience for me to treasure. Who was that infallible man on the mountain? Was it God himself? These journeys were not just a picture of what happened over two weeks, but of a lifetime. Events in the next couple of years would ultimately bring me back to the truths of God's love and my value to him that these imaginary journeys had helped me to see.

13
Tragedy Strikes

Although the weekend in Hayward's Heath had been a positive one for me in many ways, there were clearly tensions between Peter and Annette, and, I think, a lot of pain. Annette seemed to have a significant experience in seeing herself as 'a rose without thorns', but nevertheless protected. It was clearly a difficult weekend for Peter however and the turmoil within showed on his face. The darkness around his eyes and the tension in his facial expression was clear evidence of the pain within. Annette too seemed unhappy for much of the time, but was nevertheless able to enter into a lot of what was happening.

I am sure my own jealousies, insecurities and fears had not helped their relationship. My strong emotional feelings for Peter had understandably angered Annette at times, although she realised Peter would not respond in the same way to me, emotionally or sexually. She also appreciated Peter's feelings of failure and inadequacy but there was often a tension in knowing when to speak and when to be silent. I guess in some ways, it was a 'no win' situation, because when you continually feel a failure the efforts of loved ones to convince otherwise are rarely, if ever, believed. I noticed that although I did things wrong or sinned as a Christian, I was surprised by God's grace and encouraged by the way he used me to help others. At times it almost seemed as if God was allowing me to sin in order that I could understand and help others in their struggles. My ministry in T*f*T was helping me to know even more how much God loved and valued me. It was therefore an important part in my own growth and healing process. So I found it difficult to understand why Peter's response to the tremendous affirmation he was being given by the many people he helped was very different. It often made him feel even worse and more of a failure and hypocrite as a Christian, husband and friend. He would often say, 'I feel like a square peg in a round hole. I fail as a father, husband and friend!' It was really frustrating to see him in so much undeserved pain and self-condemnation. No matter how much I tried to convince him that his self-perception was wrong, he couldn't feel it. I remember him preaching powerfully on God's love and forgiveness. This certainly spoke to me and many others, but not to the depths of Peter's own soul. He never felt he could please or satisfy the needs of those around him and could rarely be convinced otherwise. These were not new feelings for him. As a child and teenager he never felt he could please his father. It was a very deeply ingrained state of mind, clearly seen when the pain involved surfaced.

The other issue I couldn't really understand then was the conflict of 'feeling like a square peg in a round hole'. He explained it thus: 'I love Annette very much indeed, but I know another part of me would love to have a boyfriend. I always seem to be trying to please people and live up to their expectations of me, rather than doing what I want to do.'

I still couldn't really understand Peter's identity conflict, because I did not share it. I could say that a part of me desired a gay relationship and a part of me did not. But as a Christian I had decided to follow Jesus and not pursue gay relationships, even though I might not always live up to that ideal. Even though there would at times be a conflict of interests for me, I could accept that as a part of 'who I am' as a Christian struggling with sin. I always felt I was being 'true to myself' as a Christian. For Peter it was very different and he often said he felt he was not being 'true to himself' and 'living a lie'. I guess it could be argued this was because he was a homosexual trying to be a heterosexual, but it didn't seem as simple as that. In fact, what does it mean to be a heterosexual? Does every heterosexual husband only have sexual desires for his wife? Peter was finding it impossible to live up to the standards he seemed to demand of himself. At the time we recognised deeper issues of hurt, originating from childhood, but it seemed very difficult to find anyone able to really help. All the ministry Peter received from counsellors, some well qualified, highlighted the issues but could not resolve them. He often ended up with an even deeper sense of hopelessness and failure. Relationships are seldom, if ever, one-sided in terms of emotional problems. Often the very strengths we are drawn to in another can bring to the surface our own insecurities. I have certainly experienced this in many of my relationships.

My relationship with Peter and Annette was proving the most important catalyst for my own growth and healing, although it often didn't seem like that. My love for both of them had already been, and was to be even more, the most important influence for my ministry in T*f*T. Strong feelings of love, not always totally pure, were empowering me to have understanding, in ways that would have been simply academic if my strong emotions had not been so involved.

No one could accuse Peter and Annette of not loving each other enough and not seeking to work at their relationship. But often the efforts of those within and outside such relationships just bring responses of hurts and insecurities to the surface, even though the intention is the very opposite. Annette's and my efforts to avoid causing more problems for Peter sometimes had the opposite effect and made the demands feel even greater, and him feel even more of a failure. We all wondered if ceasing to work for T*f*T would ease the pressure for both Peter and Annette. He therefore stopped working full time for T*f*T and managed to get a job for the local council, mainly in a printing department. It probably helped to some extent and meant their lives were a little less involved with homosexuality in others and therefore not focusing on the issue. They were very involved with the local Anglican church and I'm sure influenced its ministry and fellowship tremendously. Peter had been Director of Music and introduced new worship songs and some freedom into the worship. Annette helped many in the church and I think probably encouraged people to be a lot more honest in their relationships with one another. I was not the only person to benefit from that!

The problems for Peter and Annette didn't go away and both sought help from different people. Even so, our relationship difficulties were less of a problem now and I seemed at times to be of some help, perhaps practically, if not emotionally. On one occasion, Peter went away for a while at a time when he seemed to be reaching breaking point. He needed some space away from the pressures. Annette was very upset and asked me to pick up the children from school, while she sought some support from the local curate and friend, Ian. It was suggested I took the children for a Macdonald's and explain to them why their father wouldn't be at home for a while. This was a totally new experience for me and challenged my shyness and reserve, big time! While Andrew and

Sarah were asking me what kind of burger, fries and drink they could have, I was nervously wondering how to talk seriously with them. It almost seemed like one of those weepy American movies – but this was for real.

Eventually I stuttered, 'I er . . . want to have a serious talk with you both.'

'Fine, Uncle Martin . . . but afterwards can we have a Big Mac Meal?'

The drama I feared didn't seem to be played out the way it was in the movies.

'OK . . . but first you must realise that your father loves you very much indeed. He's not feeling very good at the moment and needs some time on his own. Do you understand? It's not that he doesn't want to be with you – he does and he loves you and your mum very much . . . He's just finding it difficult to cope with lots of the pressures at home. Your mum is a bit upset just now. You will be good children for her, won't you?' (Not the right thing to say at all!)

Sarah was silent, but Andrew said, 'Will Daddy be there for my birthday? . . . I'll be sad if he's not.'

'I'm sure he will if he possibly can, but if he isn't, it's not because he doesn't love you or really want to be with you.'

They both shouted excitedly, 'OK Uncle Martin, now can we have our Big Mac?'

The situation at home wasn't mentioned again and they seemed more obsessed with how many burgers they could consume! I was a bit shocked, but wondered if this was probably the way children often cope emotionally in these situations.

After a few weeks, Peter returned home and I thought the situation seemed a bit more stable.

I was on a speaking engagement in the Isle of Wight and phoned home one Sunday evening. I spoke with Peter and he seemed very positive and encouraged, after a good church service. I arrived home late the next day and the following morning, Annette popped into our kitchen clearly upset. She announced that she'd 'had enough'. Peter had secretly videoed the well-known E. M. Forster film *Maurice*, which was on Channel 4. Although this movie is not about the gay lifestyle (which has always fascinated Peter), it is a well-known classic depicting a love relationship between two young men. Annette discovered what Peter had done and it brought all her fears and insecurities to the surface. She had lived with the

Tragedy Stikes

fear that Peter would one day leave her for another man. Peter had also used one of her late father's old videos for recording. I think this probably made her pain and anger even more intense and she asked Peter to leave.

A fear of rejection had always been there for Peter, usually expressed in everyday relationships, rather than especially in his marriage. I guess for Peter, this seemed like the ultimate rejection. He left the house, almost unnoticed. This was easy to do of course in such a large home.

Later the same evening there was a phone call to say that Peter had been found in his car and was in the local hospital. Annette needed to be taken to Peter and in my sense of helplessness I nervously stuttered, 'Shall I pray?' It was one of those times that seemed so unreal and my simple prayer felt as ineffective as a damp squib. I said, 'Lord, please let Peter know you love him.' We arrived at the Casualty Department and Annette went in to see Peter. It seemed he meticulously fastened a plastic tube to the exhaust of the car and fed it to the inside, through the hatchback. It was in a fairly remote car park. He consumed a large amount of Bacardi and Coke and switched on the engine, having written a few farewell letters. A Christian worship cassette was playing. He clearly intended to end his life. Somehow, Peter and the car had been moved to the nearest road, with the side window broken and this is where the police found him. This seemed amazing to me, when Peter was very drunk, barely conscious and had been violently sick. He could not have possibly driven the car himself. My first thought was of an Angel, maybe supernaturally sent by God. Later I wondered if it may have been a human version, who left the scene and didn't want to be involved. Either way, I believe it was a miracle.

The next day I saw Peter in the hospital. He said, 'Did Annette tell you what the doctor in Casualty said to me?'

'No.'

He said, 'Jesus loves you!'

I will never forget that answer to, what seemed to me, a faithless prayer. I don't know how much it meant to Peter at the time.

Although Peter may not have been very positive about surviving this ordeal, we were all so relieved that he did. But now he had to face the future. Peter himself seemed fairly convinced that he could not return to his marriage, as much as he still loved his wife and children. I think he saw this, with lots of fears and uncertainties, as probably the beginning of a new start – in some ways a new life – for him. He said he could not cope with hurting people any more. Annette wanted him to return and make a new start with her and the children. For a while she lived in hope that this would happen. Peter found a furnished bed-sit a few miles away and started to rebuild his life, in the process seeking to discover the gay man he had never allowed himself to fully be. He started to 'find himself', which included buying some new clothes and changing to a new hairstyle. He made many choices and decisions for the first time, without the strong influences of people like his mother and later his wife. He met a young gay man and began his first relationship in the context of a gay lifestyle. One of our close Christian friends told Annette about this and she decided that few of their friends could remain in close contact with both sides. Some, including this person, would support Peter and some Annette. It was clearly very painful for Annette to know too much of what was happening in Peter's life or even to know of anyone close to her seeing him. I would need to have little contact with Peter, for Annette's sake, although I was able to take the children to see their father at various times, especially as the Christmas season began. Once again, the children seemed to respond quite positively, although at times the hurt and tears surfaced. I was always impressed by the openness and honest communication skills that both Peter and Annette expressed to their children – not my strong point at all! I'm sure this helped their own confusion and pain in their parents' marriage break-up. I remember one visit especially, when Sarah, as we were leaving, asked her father if she would have to change her surname. Peter told her she would always have his surname.

Annette did all she could to make life as normal and as stable as possible for the children and my father ('Pops'), and I tried to help. For a while she still held some glimmer of hope that there could be a reconciliation. They both clearly loved each other, but Peter was finding a new sense of identity and lifestyle for himself, possibly for the first time. This new sense of freedom probably made it difficult to consider going back to the way it used to be, even though there was much he clearly missed. I think, although he equated the past with much joy and fulfilment, this was outweighed by a stronger sense of continual guilt and failure.

Ultimately, Annette felt it was time to move on and she decided to leave the house and return to Rochdale. There were still many

Tragedy Stikes

friends there and her mother also bought a house nearby. She could make a new life for herself and the children, in familiar surroundings with a church family she knew well.

The children went to a new school and were asked by the headmaster about their father. Sarah replied, 'He still loves us all very much but finds it difficult to cope with all the pressures at home!' She had obviously taken in more than just the Big Mac, all those months earlier, when she seemed strangely silent and unmoved.

14
Life Changes

—◆◇◆—

PETER DEVELOPED A LOT OF NEW FRIENDSHIPS within the local gay community and found, as I had experienced many years earlier, a lot of support and affirmation. There must have been many ways in which this was a whole new way of life. Although there were still responsibilities to the children, he was also discovering new interests outside the Church and probably, to some extent, being a single person, in a way he never fully experienced even before he was married. At times, I thought I saw a lot of the 'teenager' in him he never felt he was allowed to be. I guess there were so many different emotions, including fear of the future and loneliness as well as excitement, as he discovered new likes and dislikes. When Peter was stressed he often used to find some relief in playing his piano. Living in a small bed-sit meant there was no room for the piano and it therefore stayed with me. Often, when Peter called he would start playing the piano – usually asking permission to do so! As he played, I could see by the expression on his face that he was entering his 'comfort zone', usually through playing a selection of his favourite Christian choruses. Sometimes, he became more aware of what he was doing and would struggle to find one of the very few secular songs he knew. It seemed tragic to me that, although Christian music comforted him, his Christian experience represented an overwhelming sense of failure and self-rejection. He was struggling, but fairly determined now to make the best of his 'new life'. Ever since his childhood he feared criticism. He rarely believed he could please anyone. It was hardly surprising that his Christianity was so affected by this lie. Leaving it behind therefore and making more of his own choices probably brought some sense of freedom. I guess it seemed that not being so driven by the expectations of others, maybe even God, seemed to give him space to find himself. Finding his identity as a 'gay man' perhaps seemed less painful than living up to what he believed it meant to be a Christian. There was still a lot of guilt, of course, but he probably also believed we were better off without him, which was certainly not true.

My feelings and responses were a confusing mixture of good and bad. There was a tremendous sense of loss – bereavement. The most difficult aspect of this was no longer being able to share my own spiritual journey with one of the most loved people in my life. Although it had only been for a few years, my relationship with Peter had clearly involved a journey together with Jesus. It had involved lots of difficulties and brought many insecurities and often wrong desires to the surface, but also some of the most important growth I had ever experienced. This now seemed destroyed in many ways, although not entirely. I found it especially painful to think of Peter being sexually and emotionally intimate with another man. This was clearly not justified in terms of the influence my sexuality had on those feelings. However, it also symbolised for me the different direction Peter's life was now taking, and I guess that was a more reasonable cause for my sadness. It was not always easy to completely separate these emotions, and I'm sure at times I wrongly sought to 'spiritualise' and justify them. Although in the past I left behind many relationships that didn't work out and felt a sense of freedom in abandoning them and moving on, this seemed very different. Abandoning my relationship with Peter was not an option, albeit tempting. There was a tremendous sense of commitment, but I guess also a living in hope that one day Peter would return to actively following Christ. On one of the countless occasions I prayed about this, I seemed to hear God saying, 'The prodigal will return.' I guess I cannot claim to be absolutely certain it was God speaking and not just my wishful thinking. The commitment factor has always been very important in this relationship, but there is probably some stubbornness in there, also! How do I love as Jesus loves? Not very well, I guess, when an awful lot of my desires, including sexual ones, blur its purity.

As Peter developed a new set of friends, I knew he wanted me to meet them. I should have been affirmed that he wanted them to meet me, because I was special to him. But I found it very difficult, as ever, for many different reasons. One of the problems for me with his gay love relationships was simply jealousy, as I said earlier. Another was because it reminded me vividly of the new life choices he was making. This felt just as painful. In some of my speaking engagements I had been confronted by gay men and women who expressed an anger and at times what seemed like a fear towards me, which I found very intimidating. It even made me feel threatened when in the presence of gays who didn't know me. For example, several years earlier I was on a trip to San Fransisco and found the obvious presence of gays made me even self-conscious walking down the street. I thought, 'If they know who I am, they will hate me!' A difficult feeling to describe, but the strange combination of anger, suspicion and fear makes me feel not only rejected, but misunderstood. I guess it sounds like a good reason for a therapy session? Some people handle confrontation much more positively and even welcome it – not me! Therefore Peter's new friends felt like enemies towards me, simply because they were gay, even though I could logically reason against that. It would be fair to assume they would find it difficult to understand my belief system. At least I know I would have done so, many years earlier, when I wasn't a committed Christian. I reasoned that I could make a supreme effort to meet his friends and occasionally did so, but would have to put on a mask and pretend to be enjoying the experience. I thought this was, to some extent, offensive in my relationship with Peter, which had always sought for honesty – often coming more from him than me. I tried to explain my feelings to him and he very graciously, but with sadness, accepted them. I think he sometimes felt there were tinges of biblical legalism and human jealousy involved. There was some truth in the latter of course, but certainly not in the former. I believe very strongly, that in the Apostle Paul's words on church discipline, we have to understand the restoration and redemptive motive driving them and the different situations in which they may or may not be effective. Any talk of excommunication must be seen as primarily a grace, hopefully enabling restoration, rather than simply a punishment.

So Peter and I remained in contact with each other. We enjoyed the theatre, eating out and some weekends away together, but in other ways we no longer connected. He would hardly feel he could turn to me for help and support if he was struggling in a relationship. That saddened me and sometimes made me question the practical value of my love for him, but I appreciated it was inevitable in the circumstances. Although it frustrated me that Peter seemed to have given up finding a sense of identity and self-worth from God, he was finding it in other ways, positive and negative. The scope and quality in many of Peter's relationships also made me realise how often this is missing in some Christian fellowships, especially for single people. I remember with my own gay friends how often I would pop into the pub for an hour or so, if I felt like a bit of company. I really missed that 'instant fellowship' as a Christian. I knew I could pop along to someone's home without being invited, but have always found that difficult. Maybe church fellowships should adopt a local pub, or whatever seems an appropriate meeting point? Most of the TV soaps have a pub or coffee shop where relationships are made, broken and mended. In other words it provides a good focal point. If the church is to relate to communities like the gay community, it must appreciate what they offer people in terms of fellowship and support. Following Jesus is the 'narrow road' of sacrifice, but I believe the community of mutual love and commitment that should be the Body of Christ does not mean only interrelating in church meetings and home groups.

The sense of bereavement I felt in all that happened also involved some fear. It was difficult to name particular fears, but I felt a general sense of unease. My world seemed a bit strange and frightening. It reminded me a bit of my brief time at boarding school, although I could not identify any real reason for this. I had many supportive friends and my ministry in TfT was not being hampered by the problems in my emotional life. I was certainly being given strength by God to continue with my speaking engagements and being contacted by Christians for help. I was even aware of ways in which I was being used by God, because of the situation – not in the sense of having answers, but mainly through understanding other husbands and wives with similar issues, who continued to contact the ministry. My sleep pattern was being affected and I went to the doctor who put me on anti-depressants. I didn't have a problem with this as a Christian. I had met enough church leaders who suffered with depression and knew several Christian psychiatrists, one of whom described King David as a manic depressive. I was therefore able to accept it as a legitimate 'clinical' problem. Unlike many examples of depression, mine did not involve any feeling of being abandoned by God. It almost seemed to me that God was depressed too! There was a real sense of him sharing in it with me. Like many anti-depressants, they contained some sedative. This meant that, although it took a couple of weeks for them to become fully effective, the sedative almost immediately calmed the 'nervous tummy' and slight nausea.

There was an ongoing sense of helplessness but also a strong desire to do all I could to encourage Peter's return to following Christ. Annette was settling into a church in Rochdale with her mother and the children. She ultimately married again. I was still very concerned for Peter, but felt I could do little more than pray for him. I met regularly with a friend from my church to pray for Peter, Annette and the children. One time she thought the Holy Spirit had given her a picture related to Peter, but wasn't at all sure what it meant. She drew it for me on a bit of paper. It consisted of a large key in an old lock, with oil dripping on it from what looked like an 'Aladdin's lamp' type of oil can. I eventually showed the picture to Peter, but he couldn't understand it either! I was quite shocked a year or so later, when I found an old wooden door in our cellar which had an old lock with a large key rusted in, but was still confused about what it could mean, if anything. Meeting with this friend and others to share and pray was helpful in many ways. On one occasion at Spring Harvest I even recruited Graham Kendrick to join me in prayer for Peter. I thought this might impress and encourage him – Peter that is, not Graham! But I was soon to discover an even more helpful listener, and this proved more life changing, especially for me.

I had been to several seminars on 'listening prayer' and sometimes really felt I experienced God speaking to me. This was especially vivid when the words I seemed to hear, in my mind, were not directly connected to my thinking. I guess my pessimistic tendencies nearly always made me have some doubts as to whether this was really God speaking. I then reasoned that God would always speak in terms of undisputable scriptural truths. Why, then, shouldn't my conversation with God be always aware of his listening ear and open to receive a simple response of indisputable scriptural truth? I could even use my mind to access this truth. In fact, this would be a much safer way of ensuring it really was of God and not my own feelings and desires. In a sense it was getting back to the way I used to communicate with God at the beginning of my relationship with him, before it became more complicated through churchmanship and theology.

I started sharing everything with the Lord to an extent I had not done before. My fears and uncertainties were high on the agenda. I consciously made myself aware of the Lord's presence by allowing myself to hear . . . 'It's all right Martin, I'm here . . .' 'I will never leave you or forsake you . . .' 'Don't worry, Martin.'

It could be argued that it wasn't a 'supernatural' experience of God speaking, because my mind was involved in the process. True, in some ways – but it was God speaking. It is undoubtedly what he would say. It was an indisputable truth from his Word, and therefore his words to me. As far as I was concerned, it was as real as any other conversation. Because of God's everlasting presence, I didn't need to ask him to listen – this was already happening. I just needed to make myself aware of that and use my mind in the process.

I was amazed how liberating this became. Long car journeys were the major venue for my outpourings to God. I found myself looking forward to these journeys, which seemed quite amazing to me. They provided great opportunities for unloading my feelings, without being concerned about the response of the listener. After all, he had no imperfect responses or agendas which might affect his responses to me. Previously, my journeys needed some entertainment to pass the time, usually through the radio or a cassette. I now found this noise sometimes intrusive as I wanted to be alone with myself, my feelings and my Lord. I know that may sound incredibly 'super-spiritual' and I'm certainly no Henri Nouwen or Thomas Merton. But I can say that often a five-hour car journey seemed like twenty minutes. Several years earlier I read a good book by Henri Nouwen called *Reaching Out* in which he said something like, 'We need to move from loneliness to aloneness with God and then towards community with others.' This is what I think I was beginning to experience, rather than simply seeing it as a nice idea.

This new way of listening to myself and to God was helped even more when I went on a silent retreat for a week. I had been recommended to read a book by a Roman Catholic nun, Sister Kathleen O'Sullivan. It was based on an interdenominational retreat she developed, called *Light Out Of Darkness* and having written to Kathleen, I was amazed to get a phone call from her. She said some space had become available on one of her retreats, this time in Mill Hill, North London. She believed the Lord wanted me to go on it. Would I be free? She added that most of the participants would be Roman Catholic and she usually preferred the retreats to be more interdenominational. I decided to go. I must admit it sounded less threatening than many of the 'therapeutic, healing' retreats I'd been on, where one is expected to tell all and 'work' with hurts and emotions. The rule of silence was explained to us and it was suggested we could even 'eat contemplatively', remembering not only who prepared our food, at every stage of its production, but even from whence it came. This amused me a little and I remember saying to the Lord, thinking of the food's source, 'I can cope with that if it's tongue, but I'm not too sure about eggs!'

This idea of recognising God's part in everything that exists, as its ultimate Creator, was beginning to add another dimension to my relationship with him. Some of the participants were nuns, many of them in ordinary clothes. In the only opportunity we had to share together, no one was allowed to respond. We were just sharing our feelings and perhaps what God had been showing us. One or two of the sisters shared they would have liked even more time for prayer. Considering we were given several two-and-a-half-hour sessions for prayer, each day, I found this amazing and it certainly challenged my concept of a 'Quiet Time'!

The week involved being with a group of strangers, who were obviously communicating with God in ways that I had not fully experienced before. Clearly God was speaking to them through scripture. He also spoke through their feelings and whatever parts of his Creation (living and material) crossed their paths, their eyes and their thoughts. They were really treasuring being alone with themselves and their Lord Jesus, in a way I had only tasted. As I watched people slowly and thoughtfully walking through the grounds of the retreat house, I felt closer to them and seemed more aware of 'who they were' than I had felt on those 'therapy retreats', where we exposed some of our darkest secrets. I wondered why this should be, when we hadn't said that much about ourselves, even in the 'sharing sessions'? Perhaps it was because the silence and lack of interpersonal communication actually helped us to remove our masks. We were able to be honest with ourselves and with God – and it showed in our faces.

The teaching/meditation session that had the biggest impact on me was a brief look at Jeremiah 18 (the Potter's House) – God being the potter and we the clay. The leader closed the session by saying, 'If you believe you are not beautiful, then you are telling God he can create something that is not beautiful. Are you prepared to say that to him?' I took this thought into the garden with me and brought it before God. I said, 'Lord, although that sounds great, I think if I was very physically deformed, like the Elephant Man, I would feel hurt by that remark.' I thought I was being 'Mr Kind and Compassionate'! I was shocked and humbled by God's response. 'Martin, don't you believe I think he is beautiful?' I was horrified to think I had defined beauty, or the lack of it, in such a way – and I thought I was being compassionate! Since that time, I hope I have always challenged myself to receive God's truth about my value, and God's love and forgiveness, rather than accepting anything less.

If I believe I am not valuable or not forgiven, when I have asked for it, I am calling God a liar. I have no excuse to not believe it, if I claim to love God, through Jesus Christ. I know in my case that what can often masquerade as humility is actually a rejection of God's love for me and my value. Maybe this is as offensive to God as any sexual sin I may commit.

15
Time for a Move

———◆◇◆———

MY FATHER HAD BEEN A GREAT SUPPORT in my ministry and affirmed me wonderfully. He made it clear that I was now the most important person in his life and he wanted to be there for me, in whatever way he could. Although there had been problems and tensions in the house, he tried to adapt to living as a family with Peter and Annette. They had also become very fond of him as their 'Pops'. He struggled to understand the problems Peter and Annette experienced and usually observed it all without much comment. When they both left I didn't believe it would be fair on him to move yet again. So I moved the T*f*T office into our home, next to my bedroom, with an adjoining door – not the brightest idea! We also had some 'paying guests' to help with the expenses, who used the main house kitchen. My father continued to do all the cooking for the two of us, and anyone who came to visit. The 'lodgers' cooked and looked after themselves.

I always had a problem honestly communicating with my father, at least since we had been living together. Having previously lived in my own house on my own, a part of me resented having to be seemingly accountable to a parent once again. This feeling, and the guilt resulting from it, had never really changed. Peter and Annette sometimes challenged me about it. I ultimately learnt to accept it and live with it, trying to make the best of things and not always succeeding. I loved my father a lot but could have made much more of an effort to communicate and spend quality time with him. A Burmese cat I had for sixteen years, called Misty, adopted my father and would not leave his side, even when she became totally blind. He was not normally fond of cats, but became very attached to Misty, sometimes literally. She died, and I decided he needed a replacement. He liked dogs and I bought a Welsh Corgi for him, called Vani. We had Corgis when I was a child – one called Megan was a faithful and special favourite of mine. Father was delighted, and Vani was a good means of communication between us, although he actually bonded more strongly with me. Then father had problems swallowing and was eventually diagnosed with throat cancer. I was now learning to nurse him and did the cooking, liquidising all his food. The doctor told me his time was now limited and asked if he should tell him this. I suggested only if he asked, which seemed to surprise the doctor. I knew my father had been preparing for his death for at least the previous twenty years. He spent most of his time in front of the TV and although I knew he realised his time was limited, to live in a sense, counting the days would probably be very distressing for him. I think I was right, because he remained quite cheerful, and even when on a drip for a month in hospital, he remained positive. He never asked me or the doctor about the cancer, although he clearly knew it was untreatable. I heard on a radio programme that parents in these situations often want to protect their children and not cause them any anxiety. This choice can sustain them and help prevent them from feeling a sense of despair.

After six months of living with this, father became especially weak, just before Christmas. The doctor told me this was the beginning of the end, but, although weak, father remained quite cheerful. One afternoon, our vicar, Nigel, called and prayed with him. He said, 'You know Cyril, Jesus says in my house there are many rooms and I am preparing a place for you.' My father looked up and said in a strong voice, 'I'm not going just yet, you know!' Nigel looked a bit embarrassed and nearly apologised, as if he had said the wrong thing. He hadn't of course. Peter arrived in the evening. He was very fond of 'Pops' and had visited him several times in hospital. He asked, 'Would it be all right for me to stay over? I just feel I should, for some reason.' As if he needed to ask! The district nurses, who had been making father comfortable, came downstairs and said, 'Your father seems very tired. We will be available over the Christmas period.' I was impressed by their concern. It was now about 11pm and as soon as the nurses left, Peter and I popped into my father's room. Father's mouth was wide open, as often when he was asleep, but he didn't seem to be breathing. I said to Peter, 'I think he's gone!' Peter immediately checked his pulse and nodded. We both sat there on either side of 'Pops' and prayed together, then just sat with him for a while and comforted one another. It was one of the special moments in my life and I felt especially blessed that the Lord had clearly planned for Peter and I to be there.

It was now Christmas Eve, but I was still able to make all the necessary arrangements. Peter stayed on and immediately moved the furniture in my father's room. The children joined us for Christmas, and another friend, Jane, came up from London. It was a very special Christmas for me and one I will always remember. My father had never wanted to see anyone after they died and hated burials. He said this went back to his time as a choirboy, when he used to sing over the graves of his young friends, who died in the First World War. As a result, I never saw my mother or my brother after they died. In fact I had never seen anyone in a coffin. I was determined to do this, for the first time, and went to the Chapel of Rest with Peter, Jane and two more close friends, Nigel and Linda. It was suggested that Peter and I should go into the room first on our own. It was a strange experience and although we were a bit tearful, we also looked at one another and smiled when we saw the outfit 'Pops' was wearing. It was dark blue velvet with a kind of lace ruffle around his neck. I said, 'He would be horrified to be seen in that outfit. He wouldn't be seen dead in it!'

In the family funeral car sat my cousin (and Godmother) Audrey, with her mother (father's sister) in the front seat. Peter and Jane sat either side if me, each holding one of my hands. It meant a lot to me that my relatives were able to see something of the special relationships in my life. I think, partly as a result, Audrey invited Peter to her mother's funeral a few years later, even though she didn't really know him, apart from his links with father and I.

T*f*T's ministry continued to grow and over the years a few people had joined the staff as administrators, with Sally working faithfully as our secretary. We needed a new administrator, and one of our trustees, Ian Knox, mentioned a person he met who was helping to organise his evangelistic mission in Hartlepool. This was Martin Daly and he eventually decided to join us as our administrator, moving down with his wife Pauline and buying a house in Birkenhead. Martin Daly is a gentle and sensitive man, who doesn't seem to get easily angered and frustrated. He gets on with his work in an efficient, organised way. This was to prove such an asset to us, especially in coping with my dizziness and lack of order. Pauline had been suffering for many years with Lupus, a degenerative disease. After a couple of years in Birkenhead, Pauline's condition deteriorated and she sadly died. I remember being moved when Martin talked about his last few minutes with Pauline as her life slipped away, gently persuading her to let go and be with Jesus. Much to everyone's joy, Martin eventually remarried. The house in which he lived with Pauline was very much 'her house' in terms of the furniture and décor. Martin and his new wife Ruth needed to move and told me they were looking for a much larger house. Since father's death a few 'lodgers' had come and gone, and I was living on my own with Vani (the Corgi) – a great little friend and now very much a part of T*f*T. I asked Martin and Ruth if they would consider doing a house swap. They agreed and we did. It has been wonderful to see all Martin and Ruth have been able to do to the Victorian house. In some ways, they have built on what Peter, Annette and I started. On the inside they have been able to do lots of things, in terms of décor and fittings, that we would have liked to have done ourselves. I'm sure 'Pops' would also be pleased with the way the garden looks now.

Around this time Chris Bennett joined Sally and Martin in the office. Betty wonderfully looked after the Covenants and the PAYE. Sally then moved on, after many years of helping us in the office. Chris now took more responsibility and looked after our books and literature, as well as the Prayerline and wonderfully organising our Annual Conference. Chris and Martin do much more than the office work. They support many of the people who contact us. I am continually being told by people I see, how much they were helped by a chat on the phone with either Chris or Martin. I guess most people appreciate how much we all love and value our ministry with T*f*T. It sounds corny, but it does feel very much like a family for us and many, if not most, of our members.

During the first half of the 1990s we also had an office in London. Before that closed, the staff developed for us an excellent structure for future operations, and we now have a team of volunteer workers throughout the UK. They meet with people to provide help and support, and may also encourage them to contact a counsellor from our own directory or to join one of our Barnabas Groups. Partly because many more people are now involved in T*f*T I no longer have much to do with the administration. I now work mainly from a small study in my home. I also have a caravan, in which the dog and myself visit various sites around the country. It becomes therefore, 'T*f*T on the road'. I once did a seminar on

'How to Make Sure Your Dog Doesn't Come From a Dysfunctional Family'. An American commented, 'Martin, you don't half get some mileage out of that little poochy of yours!' He wasn't referring to our travelling together!

16
Hope and Healing?

―◦―

In TfT we are often contacted by parents of children (who are usually now adults) with homosexual issues. Sometimes the siblings are in gay or lesbian relationships, and the parents wonder if they should invite the partners into their home and if so, should they share a bedroom? Many parents of heterosexual children feel the same, from this point of view, but with the parents whom we seek to help and support there are some major differences. There are usually numerous conflicts swirling around within, including guilt and a sense of bereavement – many wonder if they are to blame for their son or daughter's homosexuality. I'm very conscious therefore, in the light of what I've often said about the development of our sexuality, that I could be adding to their sense of guilt. I always try to encourage parents to appreciate how many factors are involved in the development of our sexuality and how I believe they should not blame themselves. In meetings, when addressing this issue I often use my relationship with Vani (the Corgi) as an example of how impossible it is to avoid problems with children. It may seem flippant and insensitive, but it usually helps to illustrate the point I'm trying to make. I guess it's inevitable for parents to feel some sense of responsibility for their children's adulthood, just as they do for them in their childhood. I'm therefore always relieved when parents don't seem to have a major problem with guilt. Having said that, sometimes we do meet men and women who have been seriously abused, sexually, emotionally or both, by a parent or parents. These parents rarely contact us or others for help. But if they were to do so, even in these situations, there can be a wonderful experience of growth and healing. This will involve parents taking responsibility, but moving on to know forgiveness and restoration.

The sense of bereavement or loss is very common when someone we believe we know very well shares personal information previously unknown to us. They can suddenly seem like a stranger, and this hurts a lot. We have 'lost' the person we thought we knew. The closer and more intimate the relationship, the more the hurt. If the context of sharing the secret is not one of anger, but of loving self-disclosure, I seek to encourage and affirm the parents or friends in helping them to see this. I think it's helpful to see it as 'unwrapping the gift of self-disclosure' together as a healing act of loving. In time the sense of loss can be replaced with a transformed and renewed relationship. I encourage those who want to share with loved ones by discussing this 'unwrapping' process – sometimes by 'testing the water' first through asking the other person if they want to take part in the sharing process. If they don't, then it may not be the right time to reveal the secret. Groups for parents and also for spouses work well in T*f*T. People feel less disloyal to a relative or spouse if they are sharing with others in a broadly similar situation.

As already mentioned, many people in T*f*T long to be married and have children. Sometimes a potential marriage partner, usually the heterosexual woman, contacts us seeking help for her homosexual boyfriend. Lots of questions need to be asked in these situations. For example, is the reason for desiring marriage to do with feeling more 'normal and acceptable'? We need to discuss if this is a really legitimate feeling. If the reason has more to do with longing for a life partner and children, the desires are clearly more legitimate. However, there needs to be a tremendous sense of caution and honest self-examination. We meet so many couples who have been encouraged to marry, sometimes quite hastily, by their Christian friends without anything like adequate preparation. Some of the questions to consider should be:

1. Is there a mutual heterosexual attraction? Trial heterosexual sex is still sin!
2. Is there a sexual addiction problem in either or both partners? This will rarely be solved in a loving sexual partnership.
3. Does the potential marriage partner believe the other's homosexual issues are a measure of his or her lack of love? Very important in the face of possible future problems.

Many married people in T*f*T, where one of the partners has homosexual feelings, have a happy marriage relationship. But this must not be seen as a measure or proof of healing. I am almost certainly

Hope and Healing?

biased, but I do believe many churches give the impression that marriage is the 'norm' to which everyone should aspire. I don't see this teaching in the New Testament at all.

I guess at this point of my story, you may be wondering when, if ever, am I going to share about my 'healing' – the time when I became aware of heterosexual feelings and settled down with a lovely wife and produced some offspring!! Although parenting a Corgi is not really a substitute it's still great fun!

Over the years some have suggested I am not open enough to a change in sexual orientation. They may be right. Maybe they have found in their own lives the ability to love and be fulfilled heterosexually, when previously homosexuality seemed to be their only sexual option. Some have even said to me that only the hope of a real heterosexual relationship keeps them going on with God. It has been argued that heterosexuality is God's ideal, from Genesis Chapter 2, and therefore what we should all be aiming to experience. Should we really all desire heterosexual feelings if we are not married? Is the heterosexuality we see in Genesis not very different from what we now define as heterosexuality? As I said in Chapter 8, it seems likely to me that, before the Fall, there was only sexual attraction and desire within that one relationship and certainly a complete absence of embarrassment, shame and guilt. This is a sexual purity that none of us will entirely experience in this world – in the same way that none of us will experience a freedom from ageing and weariness because of the Fall. How much of our 'pre-fallen state' can and should we really seek or expect to experience this side of eternity? There won't be any sexual problems in Heaven, for sure. Perhaps there won't even be any sex? We certainly won't be worried about it!

When I look back at what God has done in my life over my 30 years as a Christian, it is amazing. I must admit I have probably not reminded myself of this often enough. Perhaps I am guilty of accepting it to the point of taking it for granted? For sure, there have been many times when God's presence and power have been there dramatically, but more often it has been as 'my storyteller' – that is, an awareness of God in all that goes on, teaching, leading, comforting and empowering.

The problem we all face when addressing the issue of hope and healing is a very big one – ourselves! Our own desires, fears, self-aspirations and hopes are affected, influenced and therefore, to some extent, driven by our imperfect humanity. In other words, our attitude towards the issue of our 'fallen humanity' and its healing is probably as corrupted by the Fall as the issue itself. When looking at what we mean by healing and hope, we are therefore inevitably limited by our humanity. I believe that because we are unable to fully understand God's definition of healing, we therefore try to make it conform to human logic and understanding, which is radically different. Although we say, 'God's ways are not our ways' I doubt we really accept the full extent of that statement.

I believe we must start by appreciating that throughout history God's desire has been to communicate his love to his Creation. Clearly this is expressed in a multitude of ways. One of them must be the expression of his love to humankind. In other words, God's desire is for us to know we are loved and valued by him. This process of communication between the Creator and ourselves has been fulfilled through God's forgiveness and redemption in the Lord Jesus. This seems to me the main biblical definition of hope. It is all to do with our relationship with ourselves (i.e. self-worth) and the Creator, partly experienced here and now, but only perfected in Glory. The process of growth towards this ultimate healing must involve knowing we are valuable as God's Creation and learning to receive God's love and forgiveness.

It sounds so obvious, but this is something we can find painfully difficult to really experience. Yet it is the healing life-blood for most of our emotional problems. When I began writing the first edition of this book in the mid-1980s, I believed my major problem was loneliness and I thought God simply wanted to meet that need through Christian relationships, empowered by the Holy Spirit. I now realise that loneliness is usually much more than a legitimate need for other people. Right at the core or centre of our sense of 'being' there is often a feeling of emptiness – 'Who am I?' . . . 'Where do I belong?' . . . 'To whom do I belong?' I guess in a sense it is a God-created human need. It is linked to our sense of worth and value, not just to a person, but to the world in which we live. I used to quote the famous words from Genesis, where God tells us we are not meant to be alone, seeing that simply as our God created need for human relationships. This is quite correct, of course, but not the whole story. It seems to me that when God said this to the Man it was before the Fall, when Man's relationship with God was perfect. This means, even when we have a 'perfect' relationship with God, we still need other people. The problem is, we do not now have a perfect relationship with God and even ourselves, through low self-worth. In other words, we are hindered in our loving because we do not fully believe we are lovable. We are not finding our fundamental or core sense of value through the love of God for us. I wonder if it is this sense of loneliness, often unrecognised, which drives our demand for human relationships. We think they will satisfy this deeply rooted sense of value and identity, and at times in the highs of loving relationships they do seem to work. However, ultimately they often don't of course, and we return to the emptiness, maybe deciding to try once again to find another lover.

So often I, and many other Christians, have majored much on the therapeutic value of relationships. It was what we wanted to hear . . . 'You can have affectionate, loving relationships, but make sure you don't have sex!' Personally, I find it very difficult to just have affectionate relationships when there's a mutual sexual attraction. Sexual temptation is very difficult to resist. I can idealistically talk about my love for the other person not wanting to encourage us to sin, but my body can go into 'overdrive' and sexual feelings can take control. The point I am trying to make is that this search for a perfect human relationship is not the real answer for loneliness. I can only fulfil my God-created need for relationships with others when my relationship with myself, through God's love, is good and secure. One of my gripes in today's culture are those convenient, but I think often anti-social, mobile phones. Maybe it's my own prejudices, but I wonder if the incessant text messaging is sometimes a symptom of this inner loneliness I've tried to describe. I'm hopeless at text messaging anyway!

We can, however, work at overcoming the hurts and fears that hinder and obstruct this process of believing and receiving the perfect love of God. As I keep saying, one barrier is likely to be a low self-image, of which homosexual desires may be but one example in our lives. I don't mean simply in terms of our attitude towards our homosexuality, but the low self-worth from which it has evolved and which now drives our homosexual desires.

If we are to work at this process of a growing sense of our self-worth and value, through receiving God's love, this will involve learning to value everything in our lives, good and bad, including our sexuality. In other words, we need to believe that our life story is valuable. If we do, we are more likely to believe we are valuable ourselves. God is the storyteller, who allows everything to happen in our lives. This can be a scary idea, when we view it through the tainted lenses of our 'logical' fallen humanity. 'Why does a God of love and goodness allow evil, suffering and sin?' We cannot hope to fully answer that question. Our human brains are not programmed to do so. We 'see in a mirror dimly' in this life. But we can at least learn to accept it and I wonder if doing so, is also an important part of the 'healing' process.

As we begin to experience the truth of our personal value, and the value of all life's experiences, we may find that our sexuality changes, as do many other feelings. We are dealing with some of the low self-worth components in its development. However, inevitably, it is unlikely to be quite that predictable, because sometimes God's means of showing his love and forgiveness involves allowing us to experience problems and sin. It is not humanly logical, but part of the mystery of God's ways. How can we know Grace, unless our experience of sin encourages us to seek it?

> The law was added so that the trespass might increase. But where sin increased, grace increased all the more, so that, just as sin reigned in death, so also grace might reign through righteousness to bring eternal life through Jesus Christ our Lord. What shall we say, then? Shall we go on sinning, so that grace may increase? By no means! We died to sin; how can we live in it any longer? (Romans 5:20–6:2)

I am not trying to say that God wants us to sin, so that we will know more of his love and forgiveness. God hates sin and of course cannot have anything to do with it. But perhaps we are not good at dealing with sin because we are not good at receiving God's forgiveness. My experience with the Evangelical Sisters of Mary helped me to see this, although I cannot claim to have lived it out as effectively and thoroughly as they seem to do. I guess I find, as do many others, there is usually a slippery slope towards sin. I can easily try to convince myself that I can't help it. The truth is, I always have a choice not to sin. I was recently encouraged to compare sinful behaviour with modern-day leprosy in Africa. Leprosy causes people to feel no pain in their limbs but this sometimes actually results in even more disability as they struggle to use their arms and

Hope and Healing?

legs, damaging them further as a result. I know if I start titillating my desires, for example as I browse the Internet, it can easily lead to further problems and sin. I have choices to make before that starts, and if I do make the right choices there is a sense of freedom that is liberating in itself. I also need to delete the results of my sinful roamings, not simply to hide the evidence, but as an act of repentance and worship. That may have to be an ongoing process and it must never stop. The sense of cleansing and freedom may be, for some of us, enough to prevent the problem occurring, but we must never be complacent. Our lives as Christians will be a continual healing process of dealing with sins, and therefore receiving God's love and forgiveness.

I see God as the storyteller who has also given us the stories in scripture – both the triumphs and the tragedies. Sometimes, as in Job's story, it seems difficult to understand what God is doing. He almost seems to be testing Job to prove a point to Satan. Logically, it may seem grossly unfair, especially as Job is a good guy. I have heard people say, as they struggle to understand what's going on with Job, 'Well at least it worked out all right in the end!' Did it? He certainly had his riches restored and more sons and daughters, but what about the ones who were killed in the beginning? Surely the pain of his early losses and the memories of the horrors he experienced would always remain with him? Yet we have gained so much from Job's story, especially through his afflictions. We also learn so much through, and perhaps see ourselves in, his comforters. We may have struggled to offer hope and said to someone in their affliction, 'All things work for the good of those who love God.' This is true of course, but it may, in some circumstances, sound trite and unsympathetic in the midst of another's pain, hurt, anger and self-doubt. Perhaps we and Job's comforters are wanting the answers to solve another's problems and enable us to feel more valuable? We may not understand the reason for Job's affliction and know why God allowed it to happen, but we have all been blessed by Job's story, and not just the partial restoration in its ending.

We are also reminded through Job and the Apostle Paul in 2 Corinthians 12:7–8 that Satan is ultimately under God's authority as a created being: 'To keep me from becoming conceited because of these surpassingly great revelations, there was given me a thorn in my flesh, a messenger of Satan, to torment me. Three times I pleaded with the Lord to take it away from me.' Satan only has as much 'rope' as God allows him to have. But why does God allow Satan to do anything? Why not simply destroy him now and give us all some peace? Well, Paul, Job and we also, need to learn, grow and ultimately know more of God's love and goodness, through evils that are allowed in our lives. So we sometimes seem to be dealing with paradoxes, in the sense of our human understanding. God hates evil and sin, but allows it. God is in control of all, but nevertheless wants us to fight for goodness and overcome evil. He often gives us the strength to do so, but sometimes does not, otherwise we would not struggle and fail as we do. God knew when he created us with a free will that we would disobey him and he would need to die in order to redeem our sin. What sense does any of that make in our so-called human logic where we want answers to everything!

We can stop struggling to understand the incomprehensible and learn to accept it. We can work with this apparent paradox and see its value. When we value the stories of people like Job, we can value our own stories, which will involve the same dynamics. Although our stories may not be as dramatic, they are just as valuable to ourselves and to others. In this way, we learn to work with the good and the bad, seeing it all redeemed. That does not mean that we stop fighting against sin, in all its forms – both in us and in society. But we learn to know more of God's love and forgiveness. We see the truth that 'in all things God works for the good of those who love Him' (Romans 8:28). The good is for us, for others and for God's Kingdom.

How can my sexual desires and sin ultimately work for this 'good'? It may be in several ways, uniquely for each person. For example, my desires may be saying I am feeling unloved and not affirmed. What am I going to do about that, through my relationship with God, myself and others? My sexual habit or addiction may be indicating or feeding on my state of loneliness, boredom or even tiredness. What am I going to do about that, through my lifestyle? Maybe I am experiencing a 'thorn' as a sin because I have been too judgemental in my attitudes to others who are struggling? Perhaps I am a 'Job's comforter'? Perhaps I have not really understood the struggles of another, but now . . . 'Wow, now I know how they felt!'

All these have been a part of my experience and I guess will continue to be so. I have at times struggled with issues, including sexual ones, which I thought were either dead and buried or would never be a part of my experience. I'm not proud of that, but the experience has been and will continue to be a part of my ministry, and in that sense I can value them. I can therefore understand those who struggle with addictive sexual behaviour, including cruising and the phone lines and Internet. I appreciate the importance of accountability and identifying the underlying problems. My ministry has been a great source of healing for me, as I've listened to and shared with others, often thereby seeing the value of my own story. Frequently, when I felt unworthy to help others, my ministry hasn't given me an opportunity to opt out. I have then seen God's ordaining of a ministry situation, because of my own problems, not despite them. In other words I have realised my own experience has helped another, maybe through understanding, maybe because I have found (or am finding) a way through for myself. Sometimes all or none of those situations were involved, but for whatever reason I have been used. I could see it as a way in which God has certainly shown his love for me, and hopefully I have been able to express that to someone else. If that is true in my ministry, it must be true in yours. After all, we all have a ministry, whatever our life experiences, abilities or disabilities may be.

When we become Christians, it is said to be vital that we share what has happened with someone else. Witnessing to the truth in this way gives it a kind of root and stability in our own lives, as well as hopefully encouraging others. I passionately believe this is not only true for the time of our conversion. It is just as important for us to share our story with others, as it goes on. Clearly it may be necessary to share some things as principles, rather than all the specific details. I often suggest to church leaders how important it is for them to share their sexuality struggles as a part of their teaching and preaching. Following the look of shock and horror on their faces, I qualify that by saying it can be shared as a struggle with sin and brokenness. The Apostle Paul talked about his struggle with sin and 'doing what he did not want to do, rather than what he knew he should be doing'. He didn't tell us exactly what sins he was struggling with, but he knew the full details. He was therefore being honest and sharing the truth. He would not have felt, as many leaders I meet, a sense of dishonesty and hypocrisy. I guess even sharing in terms of euphemisms can seem a bit scary, but it need not be so. It is therapeutic, because in sharing what we are learning of the truth of God's love and of ourselves, we are also more likely to be confirming those truths for ourselves. In this way a theological truth moves from being an idea to a feeling, and then to a personal experience.

I believe this process of learning about love is also learning to love. This is healing based on the real hope we see expressed within the Bible. Rarely, if ever, in scripture are we given directly a hope of what God is going to do for us. Hope is nearly always expressed in terms of what God has done for us at the Cross and in terms of our redemption.

I believe we make a big mistake when we base a ministry mainly on the hope of what God may do for us in the here and now. In doing so we appeal to the perfectionist in us and may well be encouraging at some point a sense of failure, possibly resulting in a rejection of Christianity or the adoption of a more liberal approach to it. Perhaps we are even unwittingly aiding the Accuser and Deceiver, who may be saying, 'This is what God will do for you! . . .' knowing only too well that if it doesn't happen, God will be rejected. Over the years, I have seen the tragedy of so many Christians giving up on God, because of what they see as their unfulfilled expectations and hopes. We must seek never to be guilty of encouraging this in any way.

> If only for this life we have hope in Christ, we are to be pitied more than all men. (1 Corinthians 15:19)

I am really grateful to God for my sexuality, even though it has been both a problem and a blessing. It has enabled me to love and understand myself and others, both within close relationships and the wider ministry of the Church. Most importantly, it has been a major catalyst to my understanding and receiving of God's love. It has helped me in learning to know Love – the Truth which sets me free. Is that your experience? It certainly can be if you choose to learn God's way of loving. If my story has been of any help at all, so will yours.

For further information about the work of
True *f*reedom Trust, and details
of other ministries worldwide, please contact:

T*f*T
PO Box 13
Prenton
Wirral
CH43 6YB
UK

Tel: +44 (0)151 653 0773

info@truefreedomtrust.co.uk
www.truefreedomtrust.co.uk